The Aptitude Test Workbook

More titles in the Testing series:

The Advanced Numeracy Test Workbook	978 0 7494 6226 0
Aptitude, Personality and Motivation Tests	978 0 7494 5651 1
The Brain Fitness Workout	978 0 7494 5982 6
The Complete Personality Assessment	978 0 7494 6373 1
The Graduate Psychometric Test Workbook	978 0 7494 6174 4
How to Master Psychometric Tests	978 0 7494 6128 7
How to Pass Advanced Aptitude Tests	978 0 7494 6142 3
How to Pass Advanced Numeracy Tests	978 0 7494 6789 0
How to Pass Advanced Verbal Reasoning Tests	978 0 7494 6793 7
How to Pass Data Interpretation Tests	978 0 7494 6232 1
How to Pass Diagrammatic Reasoning Tests	978 0 7494 4971 1
How to Pass Graduate Psychometric Tests	978 0 7494 6799 9
How to Pass the Life in the UK Test	978 0 7494 5723 5
How to Pass Numeracy Tests	978 0 7494 6791 3
How to Pass Numerical Reasoning Tests	978 0 7494 6797 5
How to Pass the Police Selection System	978 0 7494 5712 9
How to Pass Professional Level Psychometric Tests	978 0 7494 6795 1
How to Pass the QTS Numeracy and Literacy Skills Tests	978 0 7494 6241 3
How to Pass Selection Tests	978 0 7494 6211 6
How to Pass the UK's National Firefighter Selection Process	978 0 7494 6205 5
How to Pass Verbal Reasoning Tests	978 0 7494 5696 2
How to Succeed at an Assessment Centre	978 0 7494 6229 1
IQ and Aptitude Tests	978 0 7494 6195 9
IQ and Psychometric Tests	978 0 7494 6196 6
IQ and Psychometric Test Workbook	978 0 7494 6261 1
Management Level Psychometric Assessments	978 0 7494 5691 7
Test and Assess Your Brain Quotient	978 0 7494 5416 6
Test Your Emotional Intelligence	978 0 7494 6230 7
Test Your EQ	978 0 7494 5535 4

www.koganpage.com

You are reading one of the thousands of books published by **Kogan Page**. As Europe's leading independent business book publishers **Kogan Page** has always sought to provide up-to-the-minute books that offer practical guidance at affordable prices.

Kogan Page

The Aptitude Test Workbook

Discover your potential and improve your career options with practice psychometric tests

Jim Barrett

Second edition

KoganPage

LONDON PHILADELPHIA NEW DELHI

First published in Great Britain in 2004
Reprinted 2004, 2005, 2007 (twice)
Revised edition 2008
Reprinted 2009
Second edition 2011
Reprinted 2011 (twice), 2012, 2013 (twice), 2014 (twice), 2015

2nd Floor, 45 Gee Street
London EC1V 3RS
United Kingdom
www.koganpage.com

1518 Walnut Street, Suite 1100
Philadelphia PA 19102
USA

4737/23 Ansari Road
Daryaganj
New Delhi 110002
India

ISBN   978 0 7494 6190 4
E-ISBN   978 0 7494 6191 1

British Library Cataloguing in Publication Data

A CIP record for this book is available from the British Library.

Library of Congress Cataloging-in-Publication Data

Barrett, Jim.
    The aptitude test workbook : discover your potential and improve your career options with practice psychometric tests / Jim Barrett. – Rev. [2nd] ed.
      p. cm.
    Rev. ed. of: The aptitude test workbook : discover your potential and improve your career options with practice psychometric tests. 2008
    ISBN 978-0-7494-6190-4 – ISBN 978-0-7494-6191-1   1. Vocational interests–Testing.
2. Occupational aptitude tests.   3. Vocational guidance.   I. Title.
    HF5381.5.B26 2011
    153.9′4–dc22   2010034267

Typeset by Graphicraft Limited, Hong Kong
Print production managed by Jellyfish
Printed and bound by CPI Group (UK) Ltd, Croydon, CR0 4YY

Contents

Introduction 1

1 Verbal tests 8

Test 1: Word skills 10

Test 2: Verbal concepts 22

Test 3: Critical application 32

2 Numerical tests 47

Test 4: Number skills 49

Test 5: Numerical reasoning 63

Test 6: Number logic 69

3 Perceptual tests 75

Test 7: Perceptual logic 76

Test 8: Perceptual deduction 94

Test 9: Power focus 108

4 Spatial tests 125

Test 10: Shapes 126

Test 11: Blocks 133

Test 12: Design 140

5 Practical tests 147

Test 13: Word order 148

Test 14: Numerical systems 159

Test 15: Graphs, tables and charts 169

Test 16: Memory 179

6 Interpreting your test results 188

Your aptitude profile 188
Your career potential 193

Further reading from Kogan Page 199

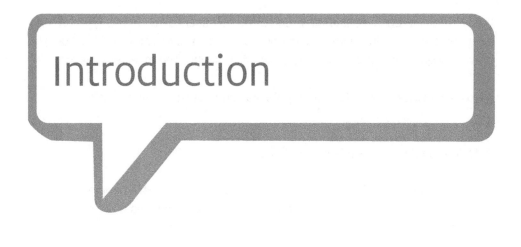

Introduction

This book contains tests of a psychological type. They will be of interest to people who want to practise tests in order to gain greater awareness of their aptitudes and abilities, or to prepare for 'real test' situations. The tests are representative of many tests used for academic, assessment, recruitment or selection purposes, and will help you to:

- get into the 'way of thinking' that is required when taking tests;
- see where you may be able to improve key skills;
- gain awareness of strengths and where they can take you.

The inclusion of two new psychological tests makes the second edition even more comprehensive. The new tests of Word Skills and Numerical Skills are longer and have a wider range than the tests they replace. They are typical of the tests that are used for selection and assessment purposes in order to reveal what standard has been attained by a candidate. They are used as assessments for further training or as criterion measures for certain jobs where specific skills are required.

Aptitudes and abilities

Most organizations as well as many educational institutions use some form of psychological testing as part of their selection or employment procedure. Testing has become routine because it is often perceived as essential, even though there may exist evidence of prior learning (school, college or professional qualifications) or previous experience (job record and other attainments). The main reasons are:

- to give an indication of long-term potential for a course, training or job;

- to give up-to-date information;

- to provide data that is relevant and fair.

Employers and educational bodies are in a position to compare people's performance on tests with other measures of success. For these reasons what tests seek to discover is:

- What can you do now – have you got the ability?

- What potential have you – have you got the aptitude?

This workbook has a comprehensive range of tests of the types commonly presented to intending students and job applicants.

'Real test' situations

Preparation is not 'cheating'. Far from it, because if you are not prepared you may not properly show people what you are capable of achieving. Too many people appear to 'fail' tests for all the wrong reasons, such as:

- not knowing what was expected;

- feeling nervous;

- not understanding the instructions;

- never having seen anything like that before;

- not knowing whether it was possible to ask a question.

There is no shame in failing something you really cannot do, but it is a waste to fail at something you can. You may have missed the opportunity of your lifetime, and this may well be a loss to other people as well.

To give yourself the best chance possible, prepare yourself well in advance. If you have used this workbook, you will have gained plenty of experience of what you are likely to meet when it comes to 'the real thing'. In addition, make sure that you do not let yourself in for any surprises. Therefore, before you even approach any test situation you should:

- Ask exactly why you are taking the test and what it is for.

- Ask how the results will be used and whether you will get the results.

- Ask what the test consists of, how long it takes and whether there is any practice material you can look at.

- Make sure you are comfortable and ready to take a test. You must not feel any unnecessary stress, either physical or mental.

- Wear clothes that are appropriate to the situation and check whether you are expected to provide any materials or anything else yourself.

Getting into the 'way of thinking' when taking tests

The tests in this book are representative samples of tests, but tests, like the people who take them, come in all shapes and sizes. What they all have in common is a requirement for discipline and attention. You can take your time and study the tests in your own way. Each is presented as a 'real' test in the way you would see it in a real test situation. Therefore, you are likely to get most from the tests in this book if you work through them as if you were taking them for real. This involves timing yourself and completing them exactly in the way that would be asked of you if you were in 'examination conditions'. In any test situation:

- Give yourself plenty of time before the test starts and while looking through instructions.

- Do not be afraid to ask questions (this often helps others as much as you).

- Always work through practice examples. Take your time and make sure you thoroughly understand the process.

- Do not start until you are ready. Do not be frightened of 'holding others up' or that you may look stupid by requiring extra time to make sure you understand.

- Work as quickly as you can.

- Be accurate (this is more important than trying to get to the end of the test).

- Do not guess (it is better to move to the next question).

Up to the moment the test actually commences you owe it to yourself to do everything you can to reduce any uncertainty you may feel.

See where you may be able to improve key skills

In working through the tests in this volume you will gain from becoming familiar with different types of test, and from putting yourself in an examination situation so that it becomes almost routine, and apprehension about taking tests wears off. This is as far as you can reasonably expect to go with some of the abstract tests, because you cannot learn how to do them in the same way as you can learn how to multiply in arithmetic. However, some of the tests do require specific skills. These include:

- knowledge of words;

- spelling ability;

- knowing how to interpret graphs;

- familiarity with the rules of numbers.

There is no reason you should not attempt to improve your level of vocabulary or practise multiplication and division. The whole point of doing so is to be able to represent yourself fairly. There is a point at which you will be unable to push yourself further, either because you really have reached your ceiling or because these types of test do not motivate you.

It may be that you prefer one of the more abstract types of test which depend less upon prior learning. Even so, abstract tests also follow certain rules and have a pattern, so that practice on these should increase your confidence with material that may at first sight look daunting merely because it is unfamiliar.

Gain awareness of strengths and where they might lead

Whether you are sitting a test in the hope of being selected or for your own purposes, as in completing the tests in this book, you should try to gain from the experience. Even appearing to 'fail' a test can be a valuable learning experience, although admittedly it is unfortunate if this is in relation to a job, place or position you have applied for. However, you may learn to be better prepared next time. You may even have learnt that, if the test is any indication of what you are expected to do if you succeed, the job is not for you!

Although most likely their intention is to be fair, some organizations use tests that are not appropriate for the purpose they intend. In such circumstances it is the tests that fail – not you – because they may not have been the correct tests to assess your talent. Although it is difficult not to be discouraged if you believe that the tests were, in this respect, unable to reveal your potential, try at least to view the experience as one that can be useful in making you stronger on future occasions. Do not be discouraged.

Remember also that a test result is only a test result. This may sound a silly statement, but what it means is that, although important, any test is only an indication; your talent in that area may indeed be higher. You may have done less well than you really can because:

- the test itself was wrongly selected as an effective measure;

- the circumstances in which you took the test were inadequate;

- your own attitude of mind prevented you from demonstrating what you can really achieve;

- you have talents that are special or different.

The tests in this volume are designed so that you can practise and become familiar with the purposes for which tests are used as well as with the process of testing. You can also find out what you might achieve in different types of test, although the main aim is not to provide you with precise indications of how much better you are on one test rather than another, or how much better you are on a test than other people. This is because the tests have not been standardized on sufficient numbers of people of any age, sex or background to provide reliable statistics. Also, because the tests are in a workbook, you may not have applied yourself to the test problems in the way you might have done in a properly administered test situation. Nonetheless, depending upon how you approached and completed the tests, you will be able to gain a general idea of your strengths and weaknesses.

At the end of the book, in Chapter 6, you can see how your scores provide ways of calculating your intelligence (in terms of intelligence quotient or IQ), and gain an approximate idea of how well you are performing. All psychologists and test administrators have training so that they interpret test results with caution. Similarly, with the tests in this volume you must bear in mind that the scores and the charts provided for you are intended only to illustrate the processes that employers and selectors use.

The important questions for you to consider are, first, which test, tests or type of tests do I feel most confident doing, and second, which tests am I interested in and do I enjoy? The answers to these two key questions may well be the same, and for almost everybody they will reflect the tests at which they score best. If you wish, you can relate the revealed potential from your test results to relevant course or career opportunities. Again, while there is no claim for precision in matching your results from the tests to careers, you can see how this process operates at the end of Chapter 6. More comprehensive matching of test results to careers is explored in the companion volumes *Test Your Own Aptitude; Career, Aptitude and Selection Tests* and *Advanced Aptitude Tests*, also published by Kogan Page.

There are two ways of doing each of the tests

The instructions to each of the tests, as well as the test questions themselves, are presented in the same form that you will encounter in tests in live situations. But how far you place yourself under test conditions is up to you.

One option is to time yourself strictly and take the test as though you are in a real test situation. Once you start the test, you should ignore any further expert tips that are provided, until your time is up. This will result in a score that will give you a reasonably good idea of your true aptitude. It will enable you to place all your various results together in Chapter 6 so that you obtain a reasonably accurate picture of how much better you may be on some tests than on others.

Alternatively you can ignore the nominal time allowed for taking the tests and work through them at your own pace. As you proceed you can make sure you understand each problem, and you will have all the time you want to study the expert tips when these are provided. This approach helps with learning, but will not be as accurate with regard to your potential, as the tests will not have been done under strictly timed test conditions. When you come to Chapter 6 you can use your own estimates of your potential to see how results are interpreted and to what your results might lead.

Chapter 1
Verbal tests

Test 1, 'Word skills', is a test of how well you understand words. Language tests are often the most complex, because a word may be used in many different ways. Words are slippery, with alternative, deeper or hidden meanings.

In Test 2, 'Verbal concepts', vocabulary is still important, but less so than perceiving what idea or association connects some words and not others. Rather than recognize the individual meanings of words, you are expected to work out those that form a 'set' or group. This test requires both a level of learning and experience and quickness in thinking.

In Test 3, 'Critical application', vocabulary is far less important than the ability to reason. While you will find that in Tests 1 and 2 you will, more or less, either know the answer or not, with Test 3 you may need to take your time until you arrive at the answer. Possible ways of doing this are explained later on.

Preparation and revision (optional)

We use the parts of speech every day without thinking. They make sense of what we say. We have grown up to learn to use them properly in order that people can understand us and we are able to understand them. But, if you are going to take any kind of verbal test, make sure you understand the difference between the following:

Adjective	makes exact the meaning of a noun (eg blue, short, happy)
Noun	name of a person, place or thing (eg shirt, person, stone, life, love)
Verb	describes action (eg ran, flew, shouted, wrote)
Adverb	word that describes how the action of the verb was done (quickly, badly, strongly, now)
Pronoun	word used instead of a noun (eg she, him, it, they, you)
Preposition	shows the relationship between one word or part of a sentence to another (eg in, at, through, for)
Conjunction	used to join different sentences or parts in order to make a connection (eg but, so, therefore, and)
Interjection	word used to express strong feeling (eg oh, ah, hurray).

Take a few moments to practise. A good exercise is to take a word, using a dictionary if you like, and put it into a sentence. Then try to use it as another part of speech. As you will find this difficult, you will quickly learn to recognize the different parts of speech.

Test 1 Word skills

This test is to check your spelling, your understanding of words and whether you use them correctly. You are asked a question and you have to find the answer from the words provided. You have to write the word *clearly* and spelt *correctly* in the answer box on the right hand side of the page. Examples 1 and 2 have been done already to show you how to answer:

Examples

1   wind   the   is

Which word needs to be added to the above to make a proper sentence?

house   dog   night   cold   fury

Answer | cold |

2   One of these words is spelt incorrectly. Write the correct spelling.

nite   free   laugh   paper   engine

Answer | night |

3   salt   pass   please

Which word needs to be added to the above to make a proper sentence?

help   and   the   pepper   odd

Answer | |

4   One of these words is spelt incorrectly. Write the correct spelling.

frend   parcel   solid   fortunate   lonely

Answer | |

Explanation

In Example 1 a proper sentence could be 'The wind is cold.' None of the other words provided would make a proper sentence with the words – 'wind the is'. In Example 1 it would only be possible to use other words, apart from 'cold', if you were trying to be poetical, for example, to create a sentence such as, 'The wind is fury'. But, this is not grammatically correct because 'fury' is a noun, while 'cold' is an adjective. Although it would be correct to use the word 'fury' as a metaphor by changing it and saying, 'The wind is furious,' this is not the word that was given.

In Example 2 'nite' is not a recognized spelling. In Example 3: the answer is 'the' because the only correct sentence is 'Please pass the salt' or 'Pass the salt, please.' In Example 4: the answer is 'friend' because 'frend' is not a correct word. In Example 2 there is only one correct spelling for a word that sounds like 'nite', which is 'night'. Example 4 is just the same as 'frend' and 'friend' are pronounced identically. Be careful – a common mistake is to reverse the position of the 'i' and the 'e'. Example 3 is the same type of problem as Example 1. Although it is likely that someone would understand you if, at dinner, you said, 'Salt. Pass please,' this is still an incorrect sentence.

Remember to write down the word *clearly* and spelt *correctly*, otherwise it will not count. Ask now if you have any questions.

If you are timing yourself you have 12 minutes for this test. You have to do as many as you can in the time allowed. Work as quickly as you can, but do not make mistakes. Do not start the test until you are ready.

1   please   clearly

Which word needs to be added to the above to make a proper sentence?

write   go   move

Answer _____

2   One of these words is spelt incorrectly. Write the correct spelling.

enquire   ofice   knock   departure   terrified

Answer _____

3   Which word is closest in meaning to 'grateful'?

hopeful   thankful   sincere

Answer _____

4   sport   swimming   a

Which word needs to be added to the above to make a proper sentence?

water   the   is

Answer _____

5   One of these words is spelt incorrectly. Write the correct spelling.

receive   wierd   fierce   deceit   shriek

Answer _____

6   Which word is closest in meaning to 'stern'?

top   front   flexible   strong   rear

Answer _____

7   an   is   a   ambulance

Which word needs to be added to the above to make a proper sentence?

road   car   the   vehicle

Answer _____

EXPERT TIP

If you are uncertain, should you guess?

Always ask the administrator. Guessing will not help you in most tests, but sometimes it is worth it. This is particularly so in verbal tests where there is not always an exact answer, as there must be with numbers, for example. It is not worth guessing if you really have no idea which of the four, or even which of three of the four, answers might be correct. If you have a strong hunch that your answer is correct, then it is worth taking a chance, but do not do it too often. Since a 'guessing correction' is applied, it is better to choose no answer if you have no idea.

8   One of these words is spelt incorrectly. Write the correct spelling.

exhausted   speady   disappointed   applause

Answer

9   What does 'dejected' mean?

quiet   thoughtful   downcast   rejected

Answer

10   illegally   is   called   importing

Which word needs to be added to the above to make a proper sentence?

smuggling   travelling   selling

Answer

EXPERT TIP

A way of reducing uncertainty is to write the word in a sentence. Then try to find alternatives for the word. Then try to substitute the alternatives in the same sentence so you can see which one makes most sense.

11   What is the opposite of 'expand'?

contract   expel   unfurl   reserve   closed

Answer [   ]

12   One of these words is spelt incorrectly. Write the correct spelling.

queue   accelerate   restaurant   business   maintainance

Answer [   ]

13   the   tower   of   Italy   Pisa   is   leaning

Which word can be added to the above to make a proper sentence?

in   on   the   under   near

Answer [   ]

14   Someone who is prostrate is...?

sitting   drunk   silly   lying   kneeling

Answer [   ]

15   One of these words is spelt incorrectly. Write the correct spelling.

leisure   thief   forfeit   noticeing   changeable

Answer [   ]

EXPERT TIP

If you do not know the meaning of the word you are given, it is probably better use of your time to leave the question and go on to the next. Timed tests will contain plenty of questions so the one on which you have become 'stuck' is not going to be critical.

16   investigation   enquiry   an   means

Which word needs to be added to the above to make a proper sentence?

the   an   hurried   telephone

Answer [   ]

17 What is the opposite of 'lessen'?

assignment   augment   greater   warning

Answer [   ]

18 One of these words is spelt incorrectly. Write the correct spelling.

advertisement   emmigration   courageous   temporarily   schedule

Answer [   ]

19 in   prepared   a   is   bakery

Which word needs to be added to the above to make a proper sentence?

on   baker   oven   bread   made

Answer [   ]

20 What word means the same as 'not permissible by law'?

indisputable   illegal   severe   vehement   deceptive

Answer [   ]

21 One of these words is spelt incorrectly. Write the correct spelling.

seperate   suppose   education   lightning   magnificently

Answer [   ]

22 of   segment   orange   is   called   a   a   an

Which word needs to be added to the above to make a proper sentence?

part   rind   peel   core   pip

Answer [   ]

23 The word which means 'to act suddenly without thought' is…?

erratically   suspiciously   cautiously   impulsively   audaciously

Answer [   ]

24 One of these words is spelt incorrectly. Write the correct spelling.

insoluble   loveable   manageable   intangible   understandable

Answer [   ]

25   a   persuasiveness   salesperson

Which word needs to be added to the above to make a proper sentence?

an   receives   irradiates   requires   the

Answer [   ]

26   The word for writing that is impossible to read is...?

illegible   illiterate   intolerable   undetectable   unviable

Answer [   ]

27   One of these words is spelt incorrectly. Write the correct spelling.

language   occasion   mischevious   disappoint   eloquent

Answer [   ]

28   the   a   sword   with   gladiator   edges   two

Which word needs to be added to the above to make a proper sentence?

is   absorbed   feinted   convened   wielded

Answer [   ]

29   What is the most appropriate word to describe preparation for an ordeal?

practise   steel   rehearse   compose   contrive

Answer [   ]

30   One of these words is spelt incorrectly. Write the correct spelling.

govenor   procession   succession   appreciation   official

Answer [   ]

31   someone   is   a   ship   called   a   steers   who

Which word needs to be added to the above to make a proper sentence?

pilot   sea   the   large   rudder

Answer [   ]

32   The opposite of 'prudent' is...?

wary   reckless   industrious   unoccupied   energetic

Answer

---

33   One of these words is spelt incorrectly. Write the correct spelling.

valueable   noticeable   agreeable   accessible   responsible

Answer

---

34   old   writers   time   often   as   an   man

Which word needs to be added to the above to make a proper sentence?

an   is   reduce   describe   poor

Answer

---

35   'Foe' is closest in meaning to...?

revolution   compatriot   adversary   mutineer   ally

Answer

---

36   One of these words is spelt incorrectly. Write the correct spelling.

anxiously   impracticable   divisible   proffessional   changeably

Answer

---

37   bone   called   the   at   the   finger   the   joint   is

Which word needs to be added to the above to make a proper sentence?

thumb   knuckle   as   near   bone

Answer

---

38   What means the same as 'likely to occur at any moment'?

punctual   accurate   patient   imminent   portable

Answer

---

39   One of these words is spelt incorrectly. Write the correct spelling.

fullness   wilful   fulfill   fully   beautiful

Answer

40   is   substances   a   separation   for   process   the   of

Which word needs to be added to the above to make a proper sentence?

confirmation   invention   regurgitation   transmigration   distillation

Answer

41   What word is closest in meaning to 'transitory'?

ephemeral   alteration   misbehaviour   see-through   perennial

Answer

42   One of these words is spelt incorrectly. Write the correct spelling.

accommodate   irrelevant   bachelor   aniversary   italicized

Answer

43   goodwill   reputation   of   name   and   is   connections   the

Which word needs to be added to the above to make a proper sentence?

value   advertisement   company   is   ordering

Answer

44   What means the opposite of 'stated in detail'?

interim   explicit   designate   nebulous   substantial

Answer

45   One of these words is spelt incorrectly. Write the correct spelling.

illiterate   irrelevant   implacable   contempory   professor

Answer

Answers and explanations to Test 1 Word skills

1	write	**16**	an	**31**	pilot
2	office	**17**	augment	**32**	reckless
3	thankful	**18**	emigration	**33**	valuable
4	is	**19**	bread	**34**	describe
5	weird	**20**	illegal	**35**	adversary
6	rear	**21**	separate	**36**	professional
7	vehicle	**22**	part	**37**	knuckle
8	speedy	**23**	impulsively	**38**	imminent
9	downcast	**24**	lovable	**39**	fulfil
10	smuggling	**25**	requires	**40**	distillation
11	contract	**26**	illegible	**41**	ephemeral
12	maintenance	**27**	mischievous	**42**	anniversary
13	in	**28**	wielded	**43**	value
14	lying	**29**	steel	**44**	nebulous
15	noticing	**30**	governor	**45**	contemporary

1 The adverb 'clearly' is confusing if used with the words 'go' or 'move' but is perfectly understood when used with 'write'.

2 Without the second 'f' the word 'office' might be pronounced 'o-fiss'.

3 'Grateful' and 'thankful' both mean to be pleased to have received something.

4 Using 'is' forms a complete sentence: 'swimming is a sport'.

5 'Weird' does not follow the general rule of 'i before e except after c'.

6 Only one meaning of 'stern' is possible from the option given and that is the after part, hindmost or rear of a boat.

7 An ambulance is a 'vehicle'.

8 'Speady' might be pronounced the same way as 'speedy' but is not a word.

9 None of the words apart from 'downcast' capture the idea of being dispirited or depressed.

10 Importing illegally is called 'smuggling'.

11 'Expand' is to become bigger while 'contract' is to become smaller.

12 'Maintenance'.

13 The tower of Pisa 'in' Italy is leaning.

14 'Prostrate' means 'lying' with face to the ground in a horizontal position.

15 The 'e' is removed when changing 'notice' to 'noticing'.

16 'An' investigation means an enquiry.

17 'Lessen' means to decrease while 'augment' means to increase.

18 There is not always a consistent rule; thus, immigration, but 'emigration'.

19 'Bread' is prepared in a bakery.

20 'Illegal' is the opposite of 'legal' or 'lawful'.

21 'Separate' frequently sounds like 'seperate' in common speech.

22 A 'part' of an orange is called a segment.

23 An 'impulse' is to act without reflection.

24 The adjective 'lovable' loses its vowel, but not the adjective 'manageable'.

25 A salesperson 'requires' persuasiveness.

26 Other words for 'illegible' are: 'unreadable', 'incomprehensible', 'indecipherable'.

27 In 'mischievous' the 'f' in 'mischief' is replaced by a 'v'. It is not like 'maintenance' from 'maintain' where one of the vowels is lost.

28 The gladiator 'wielded' a sword with two edges.

29 As a verb, to 'steel' means to harden, to nerve or fortify against something, which is threatening, like an expected ordeal.

30 In everyday speech it may be difficult to detect the 'r' in 'governor'.

31 Someone who steers a ship is called a 'pilot'.

32 Opposites of 'reckless', heedless or imprudent are cautious, wary or 'prudent'.

33 The 'e' is lost in 'valuable', but not in 'agreeable'.

34 Writers often 'describe' time as an old man.

35 Other words for 'foe' are adversary, rival, enemy, opponent and rival.

36 One 'f' and two 's'.

37 The bone at the finger joint is called the 'knuckle'.

38 'Imminent' means impending, soon to happen.

39 'Fullness' may have one 'l' or two, but 'fulfil' does not have three.

40 The process for the separation of substances is 'distillation'.

41 Similar adjectives to 'ephemeral' and 'transitory' are brief and momentary.

42 If 'anniversary' had only one 'n' it would be pronounced ay-niversary.

43 'Goodwill value' is the connections of reputation and name.

44 Other words for 'nebulous' are hazy, vague, indistinct.

45 In speech the 'ar' in 'contemporary' is frequently, albeit wrongly, omitted.

Suggestion

You could get more from this exercise if you check out where you made errors. Look up any words that you were unsure of the meaning of, or were unfamiliar to you.

Obtaining the total score

Count up the number of correct answers: _____
Deduct 1/3 of the number of wrong answers
(round down 1/3 and round up 2/3): _____
Basic score: _____
Add 4 if aged under 16; add 2 if aged 17–20 _____
Test score: _____

Establishing your level of potential

Test score	1–3	4–7	8–11	12–16	17–22	23–27	28–32	33–36	37–39	40–49
Score for potential	1	2	3	4	5	6	7	8	9	10

Your scores can be used further when you get to Chapter 6.

In careers where skills with words are required, particularly in writing, your result on Test 1 can be a good indication of your educational level.

Test 2 Verbal concepts

This test is to see how well you understand the ideas that words express. Sometimes the meaning is not always exact, but you have to find the general principle that connects different words. You are given a problem and you have to select the best answer from the alternatives given. For each question there are alternative answers. The first one has been done to show you how.

Examples

1   Which is the odd one out?

a) Fur   b) Hair   c) Feathers   d) Pile   *Answer* | Feathers |

2   Book is to Library as Garden is to:

a) Plant   b) Pen   c) Green   d) Writer   *Answer* | |

The answer to Question 1 is c). Feathers are found on birds. The other words are all connected because they describe the covering of animals. The answer to Question 2 is a). Books are found in a library and a plant would be found in a garden. The connecting idea is therefore to do with a set of things that can be grouped together in a particular place.

Explanation

The instructions to the test ask you to make a connection between words. It can help to change the instructions into your own words, so you make what you have to do clear to yourself. For example, make sure you know what 'connect' means. It can mean link or join or attach. If something is the odd one out it is not in the group or class. To make sure, do not be afraid to question the test administrator to make sure you have got the principle correct before you start. You can say, 'In Example 1, a), b) and d) are in a group, is that correct?' For Example 2, you might want to know, 'Book is in a library – that's small to large – and 'garden' contains 'plants' – that's large to small, so does it matter that the question goes small to large and then large to small?' The answer, of course, is that it does not. Anything else you are uncertain about?

If you are doing this test under timed conditions, you have 10 minutes to complete it. You must work accurately and quickly. Do not start the test until you are ready.

1 Knife is to Cut as Wrench is to:

a) Turn   b) Push   c) Screw   d) Handle   *Answer* [   ]

2 Monkey is to Nut as Sheep is to:

a) Climb   b) Wool   c) Grass   d) Milk   *Answer* [   ]

3 Which is the odd one out?

a) Carefree   b) Unworried   c) Wary   d) Casual

Answer [   ]

4 Expand is to Contract as Swell is to:

a) Resist   b) Shrink   c) Wave   d) Turn   *Answer* [   ]

5 Dog is to Kennel as Horse is to:

a) Field   b) Stable   c) Hunt   d) Oats   *Answer* [   ]

6 Which is the odd one out?

a) Ready   b) Trim   c) Unfit   d) Proper   *Answer* [   ]

7 Man is to Lung as Fish is to:

a) Gill   b) Sea   c) Scales   d) Fin   *Answer* [   ]

8 Capture is to Collar as Apprehend is to:

a) Bag   b) Sock   c) Pocket   d) Case   *Answer* [   ]

EXPERT TIP

What happens if you get 'stuck' on a particular question? Should you move on or not?

In most tests, questions become increasingly difficult. However, sometimes leaving an item on which you are stuck can free you up and prevent you wasting time and effort on a hopeless case. Also, you are quite likely to find some later questions easier than some of the earlier ones even though they may be more difficult for most people.

9 Which is the odd one out?

a) Anger   b) Captivate   c) Gladden   d) Cheer

Answer [   ]

10 Carpet is to Floor as Curtain is to:

a) Furniture   b) Glass   c) Window   d) Ceiling

Answer [   ]

11 Pure is to Cross as True is to:

a) Simple   b) Theoretical   c) Utter   d) Amalgam

Answer [   ]

12 Learned is to Ignorant as Lettered is to:

a) Unversed   b) Polite   c) Ordinary   d) Meagre

Answer [   ]

13 Pig is to Sty as Bee is to:

a) Graze   b) Pen   c) Nest   d) Hive   *Answer* [   ]

14 Mono is to Trio as Pair is to:

a) Double   b) Sextet   c) Couple   d) Duo   *Answer* [   ]

15 Which is the odd one out?

a) Face   b) Veneer   c) Cave   d) Surface   *Answer* [   ]

16 Dye is to Pale as White is to:

a) Black   b) Hue   c) Jar   d) Snow   *Answer* [   ]

17 Which is the odd one out?

a) Stump   b) Dawdle   c) Flummox   d) Stymie

Answer [   ]

18 Crab is to Crustacean as Whale is to:

a) Mammal   b) Fish   c) Species   d) Shark   *Answer*

19 Which is the odd one out?

a) Litter   b) Issue   c) Grower   d) Seed   *Answer*

20 Which is the odd one out?

a) Eject   b) Abolish   c) Withdraw   d) Access

Answer

EXPERT TIP

Is it wise to guess on this test?

You have probably read the advice on guessing if you have already done Test 1. Briefly, do not do it unless you have a very strong hunch. Ask the administrator, because if accuracy is one of the things being looked for then guessing too many times in a test may count against you. However, two guesses will not count much against you even if you get both wrong, although random guessing is unlikely to improve your score.

When tests are marked, the marker applies a 'guessing correction'. These vary, but the general rule is that in a test with four alternative answers, one mark is deducted for every three errors you make. (No marks are deducted if you give no answer at all.) This is because you could be expected to get one in four of the items correct if you guessed randomly. This test has 39 questions, so if you simply guessed at every answer the likelihood is that you would get about 10 right. But then you would be deducted one point for every three you got wrong, that is, 10 marks, so your final score would be zero. The one-third of a point deducted for each error is rounded up or down to the nearest whole number, so on this test a single error does not count against you, whereas your two errors lose you a point. Finally, the marker or test administrator might well make a note that your work has a lot of guesswork, which is not likely to put you in a good light with potential employers. Find out whether this will be the case before you begin.

---

21 Harvest is to Gather as Keep is to:

a) Spend   b) Store   c) Dividend   d) Garner

Answer

22   Enough is to Plenty as Sufficient is to:

a) Economic   b) Superfluity   c) Ample   d) Stock

Answer [   ]

23   Which is the odd one out?

a) Shore   b) Prop   c) Pier   d) Flag   *Answer* [   ]

24   Switch is to Break as Alter is to:

a) Worship   b) Change   c) Contact   d) Position

Answer [   ]

25   Habitat is to Abode as Lodging is to:

a) Quarters   b) Movement   c) Vagrant   d) Shelter

Answer [   ]

26   Abridge is to Augment as Truncate is to:

a) Humiliate   b) Extend   c) Shorten   d) Compensate

Answer [   ]

27   Which is the odd one out?

a) True   b) Fanatical   c) Burning   d) Visionary

Answer [   ]

28   Mundane is to Extraordinary as Worldly is to:

a) Supernatural   b) Tribe   c) Middle   d) Land

Answer [   ]

29   Which is the odd one out?

a) Mettle   b) Grit   c) Craft   d) Guts   *Answer* [   ]

30   Assist is to Help as Nurse is to:

a) Promote   b) Subordinate   c) Attend   d) Doctor

Answer [   ]

31 Pale is to Flushed as Sallow is to:

a) Bedlam   b) Faint   c) White   d) Ruddy   *Answer* [   ]

32 Which is the odd one out?

a) Lemon   b) Mean   c) Dud   d) Flop   *Answer* [   ]

33 Soothe is to Sore as Balm is to:

a) Pain   b) Excruciating   c) Odourless   d) Sedative

Answer [   ]

34 Which is the odd one out?

a) Confound   b) Daze   c) Annoy   d) Electrify

Answer [   ]

35 Where is to Metre as When is to:

a) Infinity   b) Speed   c) Hour   d) Time   *Answer* [   ]

36 Which is the odd one out?

a) Wanton   b) Adrift   c) Fallen   d) Oaf   *Answer* [   ]

37 Merciful is to Cruelty as Sparing is to:

a) Brutality   b) Fight   c) Pitying   d) Benignant

Answer [   ]

38 Sound is to Silence as Air is to:

a) Tuneless   b) Solemnity   c) Vacuum   d) Peacefulness

Answer [   ]

39 Which is the odd one out?

a) Humid   b) Heavy   c) Far   d) Oppressive

Answer [   ]

Answers and explanations to Test 2
Verbal concepts

1	a	**9**	a	**17**	b	**25**	a	**33**	a
2	c	**10**	c	**18**	a	**26**	b	**34**	d
3	c	**11**	d	**19**	c	**27**	a	**35**	c
4	b	**12**	a	**20**	d	**28**	a	**36**	d
5	b	**13**	d	**21**	b	**29**	c	**37**	a
6	c	**14**	b	**22**	c	**30**	c	**38**	c
7	a	**15**	c	**23**	d	**31**	d	**39**	c
8	a	**16**	b	**24**	b	**32**	b		

1 A knife is a blade designed to cut or slice. A wrench is designed for gripping in order to turn or twist.

2 The concept is what food the animals eat.

3 All but 'wary' describe a lack of concern.

4 The concept is about increase and decrease.

5 The link is with the animal and its common domestic habitation.

6 All but 'c' describe a state of preparedness.

7 The concept is what the species breathe with.

8 The concept is about 'catching'. 'Pocket' is almost a possibility but does not contain the element of 'capture and winning'.

9 Only 'a' does not describe a positive emotion.

10 The concept is the proximity and function of the article in a room.

11 The concept is with what happens to something original or unique when it has been mixed.

12 The concept is about knowledge.

13 The concept is the man made abode of the creature.

14 Multiply by three.

15 All but 'c' are the outermost boundary.

16 The concept is colouring.

17 All but 'a' are about being blocked or unable to proceed.

18 The concept is the class to which the animal belongs.

19 All but 'c' describe new life.

20 All but 'd' describe 'removal'.

21 One word is a replacement for the other.

22   'Ample' is adequate, whereas 'superfluity' means an excess of what is needed.

23   All but 'd' are supports.

24   The words are replacements.

25   All are living places; the nearest is 'shelter' but this is temporary.

26   Each word is the opposite of the other.

27   Only 'a' is 'real or genuine'.

28   The concept is what is not a common experience.

29   All but 'c' are to do with 'courage and determination'.

30   The words are substitutes.

31   The concept is the absence or presence of colour.

32   All but 'b' are failures.

33   The concept is the palliative for what is hurting.

34   Only 'd' is 'stimulating'.

35   Location is related to a specific distance as time is also related to a specific unit.

36   All but 'd' are 'apart from the original'.

37   'Merciful' and 'sparing' mean to 'deal gently with' while 'cruelty' and 'brutality' mean 'the deliberate intention to inflict suffering'.

38   One is the absence of the other.

39   All but 'c' describe atmospheric states.

Obtaining the total score

Count up the number of correct answers: _____

Deduct 1/3 of the number of wrong answers
(round down 1/3, round up 2/3):   _____

Basic score: _____

Add 4 if aged under 16; add 2 if aged 17–20   _____

Test score: _____

Establishing your level of potential

Test score	1–3	4–6	7–9	10–13	14–17	18–21	22–26	27–30	31–34	35–43
Score for potential	1	2	3	4	5	6	7	8	9	10

Your scores can be used further when you get to Chapter 6.

Test 2 is an example of a type of test that probably appears most frequently for all sorts of selection and assessment purposes. You can greatly improve your performance on tests like this if you read newspapers, articles and books that challenge you with new words and ideas. Use opportunities, particularly if you are doing a routine task, such as driving the car, working out at the gym or even housework, to listen to BBC Radio 4.

Test 3 Critical application

In this test you have to make conclusions from the information you have been given. Because of the amount of information you are sometimes asked to deal with, it is recommended that you have some scrap paper available. You are given some facts from which you must answer the question. Only one of the alternative answers is correct.

Examples

1   Pete swims faster than Bill, but is not as fast as Jan, while Jean always beats Jan. Who is fastest?

a) Pete   b) Bill   c) Jan   d) Jean   *Answer* [＿＿＿＿＿＿]

In Example 1 you should have answer d).

The problems in this test are complicated, so it is unwise to try to keep all the information in your head. Working out the possibilities is difficult this way. Instead, it is helpful to get into the habit of putting the information you have down in a way that helps you to arrange it and make sense of it. Although this may seem to slow you down, it will actually increase the certainty of obtaining a correct answer.

Explanation

For this type of problem, it is almost always useful to draw up a chart. In Example 1 it can be helpful to place the names in an order with the fastest at the top and the slowest at the bottom. You can write in the information, sentence by sentence, starting with Pete on the left-hand side at the bottom of the box:

1st stage			*2nd stage*		*3rd stage*
				while Jean always	**Jean**
			Jan	beats Jan, so	**Jan**
Pete	Pete is faster	but not as	**Pete**		**Pete**
Bill	than Bill	fast as Jan			**Bill**

2   Jo, Cathy and Sally all have two favourite foods. One of them does not like potatoes. Cathy is the only one to like pasta. Sally likes potatoes. Cathy and Jo like salad. Who likes beans?

a) Jo   b) Cathy   c) Sally

Answer [   ]

For Example 2 you should have answer c).

Explanation

The question is about what foods different people like, so it is possible to draw up a table like this:

	(People)		
	Jo	**Cathy**	**Sally**
(Foods)		Pasta	
	Potatoes		Potatoes
	Salad	Salad	

As you begin to write in the information you are given, it becomes easier to work out the correct answer. In this case, once you have written in 'pasta' under Cathy, then 'potatoes' under Sally and 'salad' under both Jo and Cathy, it is obvious that you have found the two favourite foods of two of the people. The only one left for whom you have not yet found a favourite food is Sally. Therefore, it follows that it must be Sally who likes beans.

If you are timing yourself, you have 15 minutes for this test. Work as accurately and as fast as you can. Do not start the test until you are ready.

Problem A

John is taller than Mary. Jacky is taller than John.

1   Who is tallest?

   a) John   b) Mary   c) Jacky   *Answer* [   ]

EXPERT TIP

Problem A is done in just the same way as Example 1.

Problem B

Chris and Peter play football, but John and Andy play basketball. Chris and Andy play tennis.

2   Who plays football and tennis?

   a) Chris   b) Peter   c) John   d) Andy   *Answer* [   ]

3   Who plays tennis and basketball?

   a) Chris   b) Peter   c) John   d) Andy   *Answer* [   ]

EXPERT TIP

Problem B is done in just the same way as Example 2. On your scrap paper, place the names in a line, then write the activities under each name.

Problem C

Bill has fewer hobbies than Tom, but has more than John. However, Sam and Sarah also have more hobbies than Bill.

4   Who has the least number of hobbies?

a) Bill   b) Tom   c) John   d) Sam   e) Sarah

Answer [   ]

Problem D

Jenny, Peter and Susan all go to a school where there is a uniform. Uniform is not worn at the school attended by Bill, Sally and Harry. Susan, Bill and Sally wear black shoes. Sally, Peter and Harry wear a white shirt or blouse.

5   Who wears a white shirt or blouse with a uniform?

a) Jenny   b) Peter   c) Susan   d) Bill   e) Sally   f) Harry

Answer [   ]

6   Who does not wear a uniform and does not have black shoes?

a) Jenny   b) Peter   c) Susan   d) Bill   e) Sally   f) Harry

Answer [   ]

Problem E

Joe, Mabel, Ed and Angie start off in this order of descending height. Joe grows quickly, but is still just beaten by Angie. Ed is shortest for a time, until his place is taken by Mabel.

7   Who is now the tallest?

a) Joe   b) Mabel   c) Ed   d) Angie   *Answer* [   ]

8   Who is now shorter than Ed?

a) Joe   b) Mabel   c) Ed   d) Angie   *Answer* [   ]

Problem F

Only the houses of Fred and Joe have a computer. Fred, John, Garth and Joe own their own houses. Fred and John have single-storey properties while the houses of the others are on two floors. John and Joe have gardens while the others do not.

9   Who has a computer in his two-storey house with a garden?

a) Fred   b) Joe   c) John   d) Garth   *Answer* [   ]

10   Who has neither a garden nor a computer?

a) Fred   b) Joe   c) John   d) Garth   *Answer* [   ]

Problem G

Different foods are to be found on three shelves in a fridge. Butter is kept below the eggs while cheese is kept above the milk. The butter is also above the milk, but the eggs are on the same shelf as the yoghurt. The ice cream is above the cheese.

11   What is on the bottom shelf?

a) Butter   b) Eggs   c) Cheese   d) Milk   e) Ice cream

Answer [   ]

12   Which are on the same shelf?

a) Butter and cheese   b) Ice cream and milk   c) Butter and ice cream

d) Cheese and milk   e) None of these

Answer [   ]

EXPERT TIP

The same method is used for putting items in order, one above the other, although the number of items has increased and, finally you have to work out where items go by a process of elimination. For example, you cannot work out which shelf the cheese is on by being told, 'The cheese is above the milk' until you are also told that 'The ice cream is above the cheese', so the cheese can only be placed between the other two items on the middle shelf. You have to make more deductions as problems like this become longer. Using scrap paper to put everything down makes it easier to deal with all the information and how each piece relates to the others.

Problem H

Casey, Stuart, Ritchie, Billie and Colin all have their own single tents to go to camp. Casey and Billie have nylon tents. The others have canvas ones. Casey and Colin have zips with their tents, while the others have drawstrings. Ritchie and Casey have sewn-in groundsheets as well as plastic sheets for the ground. The others only have plastic sheets for the ground.

13 Who has a zip on the nylon tent?

   a) Casey   b) Stuart   c) Ritchie   d) Billie   e) Colin

   Answer [   ]

14 How many people have plastic sheets in tents that are not made of canvas and have no zips?

   a) 5   b) 4   c) 3   d) 2   e) 1   f) none

   Answer [   ]

15 Who has a canvas tent that has a zip, but does not have a groundsheet?

   a) Casey   b) Stuart   c) Ritchie   d) Billie   e) Colin

   Answer [   ]

Problem I

Sharon, Kelly, Robina and Sam have travelled to different countries with their parents. Kelly and Sam are the only ones to have been to both France and Mexico. Robina and Sharon are the only two who have been to Spain as well as India. Sharon and Kelly are the only ones to have been to both Greece and France.

16 Who has been to Spain, but not to France?

   a) Sharon   b) Kelly   c) Robina   d) Sam   *Answer* [   ]

17 Who has been to India, but not to France?

   a) Sharon   b) Kelly   c) Robina   d) Sam   *Answer* [   ]

18 Who has travelled to the most countries?

   a) Sharon   b) Kelly   c) Robina   d) Sam   *Answer* [   ]

19   Which is the only country that Sharon has not visited?

a) France   b) India   c) Greece   d) Spain   e) Mexico

Answer

Problem J

There are five houses in Ditton Road, which belong to Mr and Mrs Bagshaw, Miss Jenkins, Mrs Chance, Mr Fleming, and Mr and Mrs Marx. The Marxs' and Bagshaws' houses have green curtains. The other houses have white ones. The Bagshaws and Mrs Chance have their window frames painted the same colour as their doors. Miss Jenkins has black window frames. Mr Fleming's and the Marxs' have green ones. The doors of the houses are white apart for Miss Jenkins' and Mr Fleming's which are black.

20   Who has a house with white curtains, window frames and a white door?

a) Mr and Mrs Bagshaw   b) Miss Jenkins   c) Mrs Chance

d) Mr Fleming   e) Mr and Mrs Marx   *Answer*

21   Who has window frames and door painted white, but green curtains?

a) Mr and Mrs Bagshaw   b) Miss Jenkins   c) Mrs Chance

d) Mr Fleming   e) Mr and Mrs Marx   *Answer*

22   Who has window frames and door painted black, but white curtains?

a) Mr and Mrs Bagshaw   b) Miss Jenkins   c) Mrs Chance

d) Mr Fleming   e) Mr and Mrs Marx   *Answer*

Problem K

Costello, Emrik, Fuji and Herz are finalists in a wrestling match. They must each wrestle each other. In all, there are six fights until the winner is decided. Herz is beaten by Costello. Emrik beats Herz. Costello and Fuji beat Emrik. Fuji beats Costello and Herz.

23   How many fights does Emrik win?

a) 1   b) 2   c) 3   d) 4   e) 0   *Answer*

24   How many fights does Costello win?

a) 1   b) 2   c) 3   d) 4   e) 0   *Answer* [   ]

25   Who is the final champion?

a) Costello   b) Emrik   c) Fuji   d) Herz   *Answer* [   ]

Problem L

Sally, Cheryl, Laura, Tom and Sandy receive postcards from friends who are holiday-ing abroad. Four of them get postcards from France. Cheryl and Tom do not get postcards from Germany as the others all do. Cheryl only gets a single card, which is from Italy. Only Sally and Sandy did not get postcards from Italy.

26   Who received a postcard from only Italy and France?

a) Sally   b) Cheryl   c) Laura   d) Tom   e) Sandy

Answer [   ]

27   Who received three cards?

a) Sally   b) Cheryl   c) Laura   d) Tom   e) Sandy

Answer [   ]

28   Who are the two people who received the same number of cards from the same places?

a) Sally and Cheryl   b) Sally and Laura   c) Laura and Tom

d) Tom and Sandy   e) Sandy and Sally

Answer [   ]

29   In total, how many cards were received by the whole group?

a) 7   b) 8   c) 9   d) 10   e) 11   f) 12

Answer [   ]

Problem M

John, Rick and Ted each have a pair of shoes, a jacket and a shirt. The three shirts the three boys wear are of three different sizes: small, medium and large. So are the jackets and the pairs of shoes. Each boy's shoes, jacket and shirt are all of different sizes. The jacket belonging to Ted is not a medium one. Rick's shirt and John's shoes have the same size label. Ted's shirt, Rick's shoes and John's jacket all have the same size label. Ted's shoes are large.

30   What size are Rick's shoes?

    a) Small   b) Medium   c) Large   *Answer* [   ]

31   What size is John's shirt?

    a) Small   b) Medium   c) Large   *Answer* [   ]

32   Which boy has the medium jacket?

    a) John   b) Rick   c) Ted   *Answer* [   ]

33   Which boy has the small shirt?

    a) John   b) Rick   c) Ted   *Answer* [   ]

Answers and explanations to Test 3
Critical application

1 c	**7** d	**13** a	**19** e	**25** c	**31** c
2 a	**8** b	**14** e	**20** c	**26** d	**32** a
3 d	**9** b	**15** e	**21** a	**27** c	**33** b
4 c	**10** d	**16** c	**22** b	**28** e	
5 b	**11** d	**17** c	**23** a	**29** d	
6 f	**12** a	**18** a	**24** b	**30** b	

A.   John is taller than Mary, so   John
                                          Mary

      Jacky is taller than John, so   Jacky
                                          John
                                          Mary

B.

	Chris	Peter	John	Andy
Football	Y	Y		
Basketball			Y	Y
Tennis	Y			Y

C.   Bill has fewer hobbies than Tom, but has more than John, so   Tom
                                                                     Bill
                                                                     John

Sam and Sarah have more hobbies than Bill, but we do not know whether they have
more than Tom or the same as Tom or fewer than Tom, but still more than Bill, so

                              (Sam and Sarah)
                                          or (Sam and Sarah)   Tom
                                          or (Sam and Sarah)
Bill
                                                                 John

D.

	Jenny	Peter	Susan	Bill	Sally	Harry
Uniform	Y	Y	Y			
No uniform				Y	Y	Y
Black shoes			Y	Y	Y	
White shirt or blouse		Y			Y	Y

E.   Joe, Mabel, Ed and Angie start off in this order of descending height, so

....tallest   Joe   Mabel   Ed   Angie   ......shortest

Then, Angie remains taller than Joe and Mabel becomes shortest because for some time Ed had become shortest and Angie must therefore have become taller than him, so

....tallest   Angie   Joe   Ed   Mabel   ......shortest

F.

	Fred	Joe	John	Garth
Computer	Y	Y		
Own house	Y		Y	Y
Single storey	Y		Y	
Two floors		Y		Y
Gardens		Y	Y	

G.

Butter is kept below the eggs, so   **eggs**
                                            butter

Cheese is kept above the milk, so   **cheese**
                                            milk

The butter is also above the milk, so   **butter**
                                            milk

But the eggs are on the same shelf as the yoghurt, so eggs   yoghurt

The ice cream is above the cheese, so   **ice-cream**

cheese

As there are only three shelves, the cheese must be on the middle shelf, because it is above the milk and below the ice-cream, so

ice-cream

cheese

milk

As butter is above the milk, it must be on the same shelf as the cheese, so

ice-cream

cheese   **butter**

milk

As eggs are above butter, they must be on the same shelf as the ice-cream, so

ice-cream   **eggs**

cheese   **butter**

milk

Eggs are on the same shelf as yoghurt, so

ice-cream   **eggs**   **yoghurt**

cheese   **butter**

milk

H.

	Casey	Stuart	Ritchie	Billie	Colin
Single tent	Y	Y	Y	Y	Y
Nylon	Y			Y	
Canvas		Y	Y		Y
Zips	Y				Y
Drawstrings		Y	Y	Y	
Sewn-in groundsheet	Y		Y		
Plastic sheet	Y	Y	Y	Y	Y

I.

	Sharon	Kelly	Robina	Sam
France	Y	Y		Y
Mexico		Y		Y
Spain	Y		Y	
India	Y		Y	
Greece	Y	Y		

J.

	Bagshaw	Jenkins	Chance	Fleming	Marx
Green curtains	Y				Y
White curtains		Y	Y	Y	
Frames same as doors	Y		Y		
Black frames		Y			
Green frames				Y	Y
White doors	Y		Y		Y
Black doors		Y		Y	

K.

Winners\Losers	Costello	Emrik	Fuji	Herz
Costello			Y	
Emrik	Y		Y	
Fuji				
Herz	Y	Y	Y	

L.

	Sally	Cheryl	Laura	Tom	Sandy
France	Y*		Y*	Y*	Y*
Germany	Y		Y		Y
Italy		Y	Y	Y	

*These must be the four who received cards from France as Cheryl only received one card, from Italy.

M.   Ted's jacket is not medium. Ted's shoes are large, so Ted's jacket must be small and his shirt medium, so

	John	Rick	Ted
Shoes			L
Jacket			S
Shirt			M

Ted's shirt, Rick's shoes and John's jacket all have the same size, so

	John	Rick	Ted
Shoes		M	L
Jacket	M		S
Shirt			M

As Ted has large shoes and Rick's are medium, John's must be small and because he has small shoes and a medium jacket, John's shirt must be large, so

	John	Rick	Ted
Shoes	S	M	L
Jacket	M		S
Shirt	L		M

As John's and Ted's jackets are medium and small, Rick's jacket must be large. The only item he has left to find is a small one, his shirt, so

	John	Rick	Ted
Shoes	S	M	L
Jacket	M	L	S
Shirt	L	S	M

Obtaining the total score

Count up the number of correct answers: _____
Deduct 1/4 of the number of wrong answers
(round down 1/4 and 1/2, round up 3/4):   _____
Basic score: _____
Add 4 aged under 16; add 2 if aged 17–20   _____
Test score: _____

Establishing your level of potential

Test score	1–2	3–5	6–7	8–11	12–14	15–17	18–21	22–25	26–29	30–37
Score for potential	1	2	3	4	5	6	7	8	9	10

Your scores can be used further when you get to Chapter 6.

Test 3 shows an aptitude for critical thinking, so is often the type of test used for selection in many high-level and professional careers.

Chapter 2
Numerical tests

Test 4, 'Number skills', examines arithmetical skills. You have to work with the rules of numbers: addition, subtraction, division and multiplication. It is also important to understand decimals, percentages and fractions.

While skills such as the rules of numbers, percentages, weights and other measures can be learnt, Test 5, 'Numerical reasoning', measures mathematical potential in a broader way. It is the most abstract of the tests in this chapter.

Test 6, 'Number logic', also looks at your aptitude for seeing a relationship between numbers. Again the mathematical rules are simple, but you have to comprehend a pattern between the numbers, which is a more abstract process than mere arithmetic.

Preparation and revision (optional)

=	equals	same as	for example, A = B, B = C, therefore A = C
+	addition	plus	for example, £2.50 + £2.50 = £5.00
−	subtraction	taking away	for example, £13.00 − £4.50 = £8.50
× or *	multiplication	times or by	for example, £5.00 * 3 = £15.00
/	division	dividing	for example, £12.00 / 4 = £3.00

Decimals are numbers that go up in powers of 10. A dot is placed after the whole number to show where the fractional part begins. For example, 39.26 means 30 whole numbers, 9 whole numbers, 2 parts out of 10 of a whole number, and 6 parts out of 100 of a whole number.

Percentages means 'per 100' or 'out of every 100' so that 15 per cent means 15 out of every 100, 15/100 or 0.15. 15 per cent is usually written as 15%.

To find the percentage of any number it is helpful to remember that 1% is the same as 1/100. So, for example, to find 8% of 345, first of all find 1% by dividing 345 by 100. This gives 3.45. To find 8% multiply 3.45 by 8. This gives 27.6% (3.45*8 = 27.6).

Fractions are anything that can be divided into any number of equal parts. The total equal parts of anything are written below the line and the number of those equal parts we are taking out of the total is written above the line. So, 1/2 means 1 equal part out of two, 3/10 means 3 equal parts out of ten, 33/111 means 33 equal parts out of one hundred and eleven, and so on.

To find the fraction of a sum, as when everybody has agreed to pay equal amounts for something, first of all divide by the number of parts. For example, suppose the number of people is 5 and the cost is £35.25. As far as each person is concerned, the fraction is 1/5 of £35.25. Dividing the total cost, £35.25, by the five parts gives £7.05.

Any fraction can be added to or taken away from any other fraction provided that the number below the line, that is, the total number of parts, is the same. For example, to add 1/3 to 1/5, find the lowest number that 3 and 5 will both divide into. This will give you the number that ensures that the fractions can be added. So, 3 and 5 both can divide into 15. Thus, 1/3 is the same as 5/15 and 1/5 is the same as 3/15. The sums are: 5/15 + 3/15 = 8/15, while 5/15 – 3/15 = 2/15.

Fractions are multiplied by multiplying the numbers on the top line (called the 'numerators') together and multiplying the numbers below the line (called the 'denominators') together. So, 2/5 by 5/6 is 10/30, which could then normally be written more simply as 1/3. Fractions are divided by turning the number that is doing the dividing upside down and then multiplying in the usual way. For example, 2/5 divided by 5/6 becomes 2/5 multiplied by 6/5, which gives 12/25.

Test 4 Number skills

You are asked to make some calculations and write down the answers. The answer has to be written *clearly* on the right hand side of the page in the space provided. If this book is not your own, record your answers on a separate sheet. In the examples below, the first and second have been done for you. Do the others yourself, writing in your answers *clearly*. You can do the sums in your head if you want to or you can do your working out on spare paper. You will see some working out that has been done in a spare space for Example 1 and Example 2.

Examples

1 How many is 27 and 54?

$$27$$
$$+54$$
$$=81$$

Answer | 81 |

2 Two people spend exactly the same amount. Their total together is £15.00. How much does one person spend?

$$15 / 2 = 7.5$$

Answer | £7.50 |

3 What is the total of 1.5 and 1.8?

Answer | |

4 What is 10% of £150.00?

Answer | |

Explanation

For example 3, the answer is 3.3. The answer to example 4 is £15.

Remember that you can have some spare paper for working out. Do not mark this book if it is not your own.

If you are timing yourself you will have 12 minutes for this test. It is unlikely that you will be able to complete the whole test as there are too many questions for the time allowed. You have to do as many as you can, working quickly, but not making mistakes. Do not start the test until you are ready.

1   How many is 13 and 8?

Answer [   ]

2   Two people spend £6.00 each. How much did they spend together?

Answer [   ]

3   What is the total of 0.5 and 1.0?

Answer [   ]

EXPERT TIP

When adding decimals, place the decimal points of all the numbers under each other. This makes sure that tens of units come under each other, units come under each other, as well as tenths, hundredths, thousandths and so on. So if you need to add, say, 3.08 and 10.003 and 4.94, write the sum down as below. Add the numbers from the right-hand side in the normal way:

$$
\begin{array}{r}
3.08 \\
+ \ 10.003 \\
+ \ \underline{4.94} \\
= 18.023
\end{array}
$$

---

4   What is 50% of £10.00?

Answer [   ]

5   How many is 16 added to 23?

Answer [   ]

6   What does £9.50 and £10.50 come to?

Answer [   ]

7   What is the total of 1½ and 1½ ?

Answer [   ]

8   What is 25% of £40.00?

Answer

9   What is 39 plus 28?

Answer

10   What is the total if two people each spend £10.75?

Answer

11   Two people each decide to pay ½ of £180.00. What did one person pay?

Answer

12   What is 30% of £150.00?

Answer

13   What is 88 and 69?

Answer

14   What does £133.00 and £96.00 come to?

Answer

15   What is the total of 3½ and 4½ ?

Answer

EXPERT TIP

50% is the same as saying '50 parts out of 100', which is the same as saying 'a half' or '½'. 25% is the same as saying 'a quarter'. In Question 8, dividing £40.00 by 4 gives £10.00. This is probably the simplest way. Alternatively, you could find 10% (or 10 parts out of a hundred) of £40.00, which is £4.00, then multiply by 25, or you could find 1% (or 1 part out of 100) of £40.00, which is 0.4, then multiply by 25.

16   What is 7% of £300.00?   *Answer* [   ]

17   What is the total of these numbers: 161 plus 278 plus 93?

                                                              Answer [   ]

18   What is the total of the following: £5.90, £6.20, £3.85?

                                                              Answer [   ]

19   What is ¼ of £84.00?   *Answer* [   ]

20   How much does a £255.00 item cost when sold for 10% less?

                                                              Answer [   ]

21   What is 1045 less 109?   *Answer* [   ]

22   What is left if £35.55 is taken from £50.00?

                                                              Answer [   ]

23   What is a fifth share of £950.00?   *Answer* [   ]

24   If 35% of an item cost £140.00, what was the full cost?

                                                              Answer [   ]

25   What is twice 138 taken away from 454?

                                                              Answer [   ]

26   How many complete items at £3.50 each can be bought from £28.00?

                                                              Answer [   ]

27   What is 2¾ multiplied by 3?

                                                              Answer [   ]

EXPERT TIP

To multiply fractions, you multiply the numbers above the bar together, then multiply the numbers below the bar together. Suppose you had to multiply 1½ × 1¾ × 2½ . First of all, change all the numbers so they become fractions (these are called 'improper fractions'), then multiply the numbers above the line (called 'numerators') and the numbers below the line (called 'denominators).

$$1½ × 1¾ × 2½ = \frac{3 × 7 × 5}{2 × 4 × 4} = \frac{105}{32} = 3 \text{ and } ⁹/₃₂$$

28   What is paid if an item costing £880.00 has a 2½ % discount?

Answer

29   How many groups of 5 are there in 70?   *Answer*

30   How much is left from £29.27 after deducting £13.75?

Answer

31   What is one third multiplied by ½ ?   *Answer*

EXPERT TIP

To divide fractions, you change the fraction that is doing the dividing up the other way. For example, let us take 1/8 divided by 4:

$$\frac{1}{8} / \frac{4}{1} = \frac{1}{8} × \frac{1}{4} = \frac{1}{32}$$

Remember, division is the inverse or opposite of multiplication. You always invert the number that is doing the dividing, so to divide a number by 3/4 you multiply by 4/3. To divide by one and four fifths or 1 and 4/5, you first make the whole number an improper fraction, which is 9/5, and then multiply by 5/9.

32   What is the interest on £600.00 at 5% annually?

Answer [   ]

33   What number divides 93 to give the result of 3?

Answer [   ]

34   What is 2.95 divided by 0.05?

Answer [   ]

EXPERT TIP

To divide decimals first make the number that is doing the dividing (called the 'divisor') into a whole number. In Question 34 this is done by moving the decimal point two places to the right, which is 5.0, a whole number. What you do to one number must also be done to the other so that 2.95 becomes 295. Now divide 5 into 295 in the normal way.

35   If one share costs £8.00, what is the cost of 3½ shares plus 2¼ shares?

Answer [   ]

36   What is 1% of £10.00 added to 2% of £100.00?

Answer [   ]

37   What has to be added to 1003 to give 2171?

Answer [   ]

38   If 20 parts cost £1000.00, how much is 5½ parts?

Answer [   ]

39   What is 1/5 less 1/15 ?

Answer [   ]

40 What is 17½ % of £50.00?

Answer

41 Making up sets of 12, how many will be left over from a group of 165?

Answer

42 If there are 250 rials to the pound sterling, how many pounds sterling can be bought for 5000.00 (five thousand) rials?

Answer

Answers and explanations to Test 4
Number skills

1	21	**10**	£21.50	**19**	21	**28**	£858.00	**37**	1168
2	£12.00	**11**	£90.00	**20**	£229.50	**29**	14	**38**	£275.00
3	1.5	**12**	£45.00	**21**	936	**30**	£15.52	**39**	2/15
4	£5.00	**13**	157	**22**	£14.45	**31**	1/6	**40**	£8.75
5	39	**14**	£229.00	**23**	£190.00	**32**	£30.00	**41**	9
6	£20.00	**15**	8	**24**	£400.00	**33**	31	**42**	£20.00
7	3	**16**	£21.00	**25**	178	**34**	59		
8	£10.00	**17**	532	**26**	8	**35**	£46.00		
9	67	**18**	£15.95	**27**	8 1/4	**36**	£2.10		

1
$$\begin{array}{r} 13 \\ + 8 \\ \hline 21 \end{array}$$

2
$$\begin{array}{r} 6 \\ \times 2 \\ \hline 12 \end{array}$$

3
$$\begin{array}{r} 0.5 \\ + 1.0 \\ \hline 1.5 \end{array}$$

4
$$50\% \text{ of } £10.00 = £10 \times \frac{50}{100} = \frac{500}{100} = £5$$

5
$$\begin{array}{r} 16 \\ + 23 \\ \hline 39 \end{array}$$

6
$$\begin{array}{r} 9.50 \\ + 10.50 \\ \hline 20.00 \end{array}$$

7
$$1\frac{1}{2} + 1\frac{1}{2} = 2 + \frac{1}{2} + \frac{1}{2} = 2 + \frac{2}{2} = 2 + \frac{1}{1} = 3$$

8 $25\% \text{ of } £40.00 = £40 \times \dfrac{25}{100} = \dfrac{1000}{100} = £10$

9
$$\begin{array}{r} 39 \\ + 28 \\ \hline 67 \end{array}$$

10
$$\begin{array}{r} 10.75 \\ \times \ 2.0 \\ \hline 21.50 \end{array}$$

11 $\dfrac{1}{2} \text{ of } £180 = \dfrac{1}{2} \times \dfrac{180}{1} = \dfrac{180}{2} = £90$

12 $30\% \text{ of } £150.00 = \dfrac{30}{100} \times \dfrac{150}{1} = \dfrac{4500}{100} = £45$

13
$$\begin{array}{r} 88 \\ + \ 69 \\ \hline 157 \end{array}$$

14
$$\begin{array}{r} 133.00 \\ + \ 96.00 \\ \hline 229.00 \end{array}$$

15 $3\dfrac{1}{2} + 4\dfrac{1}{2} = 7 + \dfrac{1}{2} + \dfrac{1}{2} = 7 + \dfrac{2}{2} = 7 + \dfrac{1}{1} = 8$

16 $7\% \text{ of } £300.00 = \dfrac{7}{100} \times \dfrac{300}{1} = \dfrac{2100}{100} = \dfrac{21}{1} = £21$

17
$$\begin{array}{r} 161 \\ 278 \\ 93 \\ \hline 532 \end{array}$$

18
$$\begin{array}{r} 5.90 \\ 6.20 \\ 3.85 \\ \hline 15.95 \end{array}$$

19

$$\frac{1}{4} \text{ of } 84 = \frac{1}{4} \times \frac{84}{1} = \frac{84}{4} = \frac{21}{1} = 21$$

20

$$90\% \text{ of } £255.00 = \frac{90}{100} \times \frac{255}{1} = \frac{9}{10} \times \frac{255}{1} = \frac{9}{2} \times \frac{51}{1} = \frac{459}{2} = £229.50$$

21

$$\begin{array}{r} 1045 \\ - \ 109 \\ \hline 936 \end{array}$$

22

$$\begin{array}{r} 50.00 \\ - \ 35.55 \\ \hline 14.45 \end{array}$$

23

$$\frac{1}{5} \text{ of } £950 = \frac{1}{5} \times \frac{950}{1} = \frac{950}{5} = \frac{190}{1} = £190$$

24

$$35\% \text{ cost } £140 \text{ so full cost is } = \frac{100}{35} \times \frac{140}{1} = \frac{20}{7} \times \frac{140}{1}$$

$$= \frac{20}{1} \times \frac{20}{1} = \frac{400}{1} = £400$$

Or, since 7 will divide into both 35 and 140, 7 into 35 gives 7, and 7 divides into 140 giving 20. Therefore, 5% of the full cost is £20. The full cost is 20 times £20 (20 x 5% is %100) = £400

25

$$\begin{array}{r} 138 \\ + \ 138 \\ \hline 276 \end{array} \qquad \begin{array}{r} 454 \\ - \ 276 \\ \hline 178 \end{array}$$

26

$$£28 \div £3.50 = 28 \div 3\frac{1}{2} = \frac{28}{1} \div \frac{7}{2} = \frac{28}{1} \times \frac{2}{7} = \frac{56}{7} = 8$$

Or $\qquad 3.5\overline{)28.00}$

then

$$\begin{array}{r} 8.00 \\ 35\overline{)280.00} \\ 280 \end{array}$$

27 $\quad 2\dfrac{3}{4} \times 3 = 2\dfrac{3}{4} \times \dfrac{3}{1} = \dfrac{11}{4} \times \dfrac{3}{1} = \dfrac{33}{4} = 8\dfrac{1}{4}$

28 $\quad$ 2 ½ % is a ¼ of 10 %. 10% of £880.00 is £88.00. A ¼ of this is £22.00. £880.00 less £22.00 is £858.00.

29

$$
\begin{array}{r}
14.00 \\
5\overline{)70.00} \\
\underline{5} \\
20. \\
\underline{0.00}
\end{array}
$$

30

$$
\begin{array}{r}
29.27 \\
-13.75 \\
\hline
15.52 \\
\hline
\end{array}
$$

31 $\quad \dfrac{1}{3} \times \dfrac{1}{2} = \dfrac{1}{6}$

32 $\quad £600 \times 5\% = \dfrac{600}{1} \times \dfrac{5}{100} = \dfrac{6}{1} \times \dfrac{5}{1} = \dfrac{30}{1} = £30.00$

33

$$
\begin{array}{r}
31.00 \\
3\overline{)93.00} \\
\underline{9} \\
3 \\
\underline{3}
\end{array}
$$

34 $\quad 0.05\overline{)2.95}$

$$
5\overline{)295.0}
$$

$$
\begin{array}{r}
59.0 \\
5\overline{)295.0} \\
\underline{25} \\
45 \\
\underline{45}
\end{array}
$$

35

$$£8.00 \times (3\frac{1}{2} + 2\frac{1}{4})$$

$$= £8.00 \times (5 + \frac{1}{2} + \frac{1}{4})$$

$$= £8.00 \times (5 + \frac{2}{4} + \frac{1}{4})$$

$$= £8.00 \times 5\frac{3}{4}$$

$$= \frac{8}{1} \times \frac{23}{4} = \frac{2}{1} \times \frac{23}{1} = \frac{46}{1} = £46.00$$

36 1% of £10 can be found by, firstly, 10% of £10, which is £1.00, and then another 10% of that, which is 10 pence. 2% of £100.00 can be found by, firstly, 10% of £100, which is £10, and then 20% (or one fifth) of that, which is £2.00. The answer is therefore the sum of the two, which is £2.10.

37   2171
       − 1003
       ‾‾‾‾‾
        1168

38 Find one part by dividing 20 into £1000.00, which is £50. 5 ½ parts cost 5 ½ times 50, which is £275.

39

$$\frac{1}{5} - \frac{1}{15}$$

$$= \frac{3}{15} - \frac{1}{15} = \frac{2}{15}$$

40 10 % of £50 is £5. This represents 2 ½ times 4 parts, where each part is £1.25. 7 parts (7 parts out of 40 is the same as 17 ½ %), is £1.25 times 7, which is £8.75.

41   13.0
       12)165.0
          12
          ‾‾
          45
          36
          ‾‾
           9 remaining

42   250 rials go into 5000 rials 20 times, so five thousand rials would cost £20.00.

$$(\frac{1}{100} \times \frac{10}{1}) + (\frac{2}{100} \times \frac{100}{1})$$

$$= (\frac{1}{10} \times \frac{1}{1}) + (\frac{2}{1} \times \frac{1}{1})$$

$$= (\frac{1}{10}, \text{which is } 10 \text{ pence}) + (\frac{2}{1}, \text{which is } £2)$$

$$= £2.10$$

Obtaining the total score

Count up the number of correct answers: _____

Deduct 1/4 of the number of wrong answers
(round down 1/4 and ½, round up 3/4):   _____

Basic score: _____

Add 2 if no mistakes: _____

Test score: _____

Establishing your level of potential

Test score	1–2	3–4	5–8	9–12	13–16	17–20	21–25	26–30	31–35	36–44
Score for potential	1	2	3	4	5	6	7	8	9	10

Your scores can be used further when you get to Chapter 6.

If you do well in Test 4 and enjoy arithmetic and other problems involving calculations you may want to consider careers that have a strong numerical element, such as those in accountancy, finance, administration and economics.

Test 5 Numerical reasoning

This is a test of how easily you perceive how numbers relate to each other. You are given a series of numbers. You then have to choose the number that would go next in the series, choosing one from the four possible answers provided. It is advisable to have a piece of scrap paper and a pencil to do any working out that may be necessary. The first example below has been done already to show you how.

Examples

1   5   10   15   20   25   ?
   a) 6   b) 35   c) 30   d) 50   *Answer*   [30]

2   15   12.5   10   7.5   5   ?
   a) 2.5   b) 5   c) 1   d) 0   *Answer*   [   ]

3   2   5   11   23   47   ?
   a) 70   b) 57   c) 58   d) 95   *Answer*   [   ]

The answer to Example 1 is c) because the numbers are a series increasing by 5.

   The answer to Example 2 is a) because the series is reducing by 2.5, so you should take 2.5 away from 5.

   The answer to Example 3 is d) because the gaps between the numbers are 3, 6, 12 and 24, so 48 is needed to fill the gap between the last and missing number. So, 48 added to 47 is 95. Alternatively, this series can be done by doubling each of the numbers in the series and adding 1.

If you are timing yourself you have 10 minutes to do as much as you can. You must work as quickly and as accurately as possible. Do not start until you are ready.

1   3   7   11   15   19   ?

    a) 21   b) 23   c) 25   d) 27   *Answer*

2   ¼   ½   1   2   4   ?

    a) 12   b) 16   c) 8   d) 10   *Answer*

3   0   1   3   7   15   ?

    a) 11   b) 35   c) 21   d) 31   *Answer*

EXPERT TIP

So far, the problems have been simple increasing series where the same amount or twice the same amount is added each time. Descending series work in exactly the same way.

4   3   3   6   9   15   ?

    a) 20   b) 21   c) 18   d) 24   *Answer*

EXPERT TIP

Problem 5 is a 'step up' in terms of complication because the answer is not given by working out the connection between the numbers, but more between the spaces between the numbers. This is when it becomes almost essential to have scrap paper in order that you can try out various combinations. In the example above:

      6   10   14   18   22?   (4 is added each time)

      2 8 18 32 50 (and 72 is a possible answer)

5   2   8   18   32   50   ?

    a) 60   b) 64   c) 72   d) 70   *Answer*

6   2304   576   144   36   9   ?

     a) 3   b) 9   c) 2 1/4   d) 4   *Answer*

7   0.02   0.04   0.06   0.08   0.1   ?

     a) 0.12   b) 0.102   c) 1.02   d) 0.03   *Answer*

8   1   3   6   10   15   ?

     a) 20   b) 21   c) 25   d) 30   *Answer*

9   1   5   9   13   17   ?

     a) 24   b) 23   c) 22   d) 21   *Answer*

10   0   3   7   12   18   ?

     a) 24   b) 29   c) 25   d) 34   *Answer*

11   287   143   71   35   17   ?

     a) 8   b) 18   c) 11   d) 7   *Answer*

12   1   2   5   10   17   ?

     a) 30   b) 29   c) 27   d) 26   *Answer*

13   4   7   6   9   8   ?

     a) 16   b) 11   c) 13   d) 10   *Answer*

EXPERT TIP

You must be alert to ascending and descending series operating at the same time.
In Question 13 it is helpful to use some scrap paper to see what possibilities there might be:

         +3   +3   +3   ?

           4   7   6   9   8   (and 11 is a possible answer)

              −1   −1

14   1   9   10   19   29   ?

    a) 48   b) 39   c) 38   d) 58   *Answer*

15   0   11   11   22   33   ?

    a) 44   b) 55   c) 33   d) 22   *Answer*

16   7   14   10   24   16   ?

    a) 26   b) 34   c) 40   d) 37   *Answer*

EXPERT TIP

There may be more than one answer to the series, but look for the simplest possible answer from those alternatives provided. For example, in Question 16:

   +7   +14   +28? or +21?   (double the number or add 7)

7   14   10   24   16   ?

         −4   −8   (44 is not a possible answer but 37 is)

17   2   4   3   7   6   ?

    a) 9   b) 13   c) 15   d) 14   *Answer*

18   100   60   120   80   140   ?

    a) 220   b) 120   c) 100   d) 160   *Answer*

19   3   9   9   27   27   ?

    a) 54   b) 36   c) 243   d) 81   *Answer*

20   13   9   22   31   53   ?

    a) 75   b) 84   c) 106   d) 62   *Answer*

21   2   3   7   17   39   ?

    a) 58   b) 85   c) 65   d) 75   *Answer*

Answers and explanations to Test 5
Numerical reasoning

1	b	**7**	a	**12**	d	**17**	d
2	c	**8**	b	**13**	b	**18**	c
3	d	**9**	d	**14**	a	**19**	d
4	d	**10**	c	**15**	b	**20**	b
5	c	**11**	a	**16**	d	**21**	b
6	c						

1 Series ascends by 4.
2 Series doubles.
3 Differences between numbers doubles.
4 Each number is the total of the two numbers that precede it.
5 Difference between the numbers increases by 4.
6 Descending numbers are a quarter of the preceding number.
7 Each number is increased by 0.02.
8 Differences between the numbers increase by 1.
9 Numbers ascend by adding 4.
10 Differences between numbers increase by 1.
11 One is taken from the number and divided by 2.
12 Differences between numbers cannot be divided by any other number (prime numbers).
13 Successively add 3 minus 1.
14 Each number is an addition of the two previous numbers.
15 Each number is an addition of the two previous numbers.

18 Two series. One, in which successive numbers decline by 20, and a second in Which successive numbers rise by 20.

19 $(3 \times 3 = 9)$ $(9 \times 3 = 27)$ $(27 \times 3 = 81)$.

20		13		9		22		31	
13		9		22		31		53		84
	−4		13		9		22		31

21		1		4		10		22		46	
2		3		7		17		39		85

Numbers in the 'top line' are doubled and have two added.

Obtaining the total score

Count up the number of correct answers: _____

Deduct 1/3 of the number of wrong answers
(round down 1/3, round up 2/3):   _____

Basic score: _____

Add 2 if no mistakes: _____

Test score: _____

Establishing your level of potential

Test score	1	2	3–4	5–7	8–10	11–13	14–15	16–17	18–19	20–23
Score for potential	1	2	3	4	5	6	7	8	9	10

Your scores can be used further when you get to Chapter 6.

Proficiency with Test 5, 'Numerical reasoning', would be proof of numerical strengths that could take you into careers connected with econometrics, actuarial work, as well as broader areas connected with mathematics, such as science and technology.

Test 6 Number logic

This test examines how quickly you can see a relationship between different pairs of numbers. You are given five pairs of numbers. Two of the pairs have a relationship. You have to find the pairs that go together. The example below has been done already to show you how.

Example

3:3 4:1 9:3 1:5 1:3

a   b   c   d   e

Answer   c, e

The answer is 'c and e' because 1:3 goes with 9:3. The larger figure is 3 times the smaller figure. So 1 is to 3, as 3 is to 9. The fact that the numbers are around the other way does not matter. Sometimes the numbers are the same way, sometimes they are not. No other pair would be logical.

When you find the correct answer, write in the box in the same way as in the example. You may find it helpful to have a piece of scrap paper. Try the following for yourself.

1   2:1   3:7   1:2   4:1   5:3

a   b   c   d   e   *Answer*

2   5:4   1:3   1:5   3:2   3:9

a   b   c   d   e   *Answer*

3   1:5   3:4   7:3   5:2   6:14

a   b   c   d   e   *Answer*

The answer to Example 1 is 'a and c'. (2 is to 1 is the same as 1 is to 2.)

The answer to Example 2 is 'b and e' because the larger number in both pairs is 3 times the smaller number. (1 is to 3 is the same as 3 is to 9.)

In the third example, the answer is 'c and e' because one pair is twice the other pair. (7 is half of 14, 3 is half of 6.)

Work as quickly and accurately as you can. Do not guess, because that counts against you. You have 10 minutes. Do not start the test until you are ready.

1　a) 2:2　　b) 5:1　　c) 1:4　　d) 3:1　　e) 1:1

Answer _____

2　a) 4:1　　b) 12:6　　c) 2:1　　d) 5:4　　e) 7:1

Answer _____

3　a) 1:6　　b) 4:3　　c) 5:1　　d) 6:18　　e) 1:3

Answer _____

4　a) 36:6　　b) 4:5　　c) 8:40　　d) 6:1　　e) 2:20

Answer _____

EXPERT TIP

It is difficult to work with big numbers. Always try to make the numbers as small as you can, which makes it easier to see the relationship with another number. In the first place try to divide the smaller number of the pair into the larger one. For example, in Question 4, 36:6 divided by 6, gives you 6:1, which makes a pair with answer d).

　　To reduce numbers to a manageable size remember that any pair of numbers that are even can always be divided by 2. If one or both of a pair is odd it cannot be divided by 2, so try 3, then 5, 7, and so on until your divisor is too large to go into either number.

5　a) 4:10　　b) 9:2　　c) 3:1　　d) 5:2　　e) 6:1

Answer _____

6　a) 10:7　　b) 5:3　　c) 2:16　　d) 9:3　　e) 9:15

Answer _____

7　a) 18:3　　b) 1:6　　c) 1:4　　d) 2:2　　e) 21:7

Answer _____

EXPERT TIP

You can improve your performance on this type of test by practising your 'times tables'. When you have a spare moment, simply take a number, say, any number from 1 to 15, and count up in multiples of that number. Another good exercise to do in your head is to take a small number, such as 2, and keep doubling it.

8   a) 12:2   b) 14:2   c) 8:3   d) 6:42   e) 30:4

Answer _____

9   a) 2:1   b) 4:1   c) 3:4   d) 1:5   e) 10:6   f) 4:8

Answer _____

10   a) 12:4   b) 2:4   c) 5:3   d) 15:9   e) 12:2   f) 1:12

Answer _____

11   a) 5:9   b) 8:12   c) 4:2   d) 3:1   e) 1:4   f) 15:27

Answer _____

12   a) 13:1   b) 25:5   c) 26:4   d) 52:3   e) 3:39   f) 40:50

Answer _____

13   a) 12:4   b) 8:64   c) 9:15   d) 10:2   e) 22:11   f) 25:5

Answer _____

14   a) 63:7   b) 2:9   c) 5:1   d) 35:7   e) 10:11   f) 7:1

Answer _____

15   a) 8:7   b) 12:6   c) 21:24   d) 7:6   e) 7:10   f) 6:4

Answer _____

16 a) 10:42   b) 5:12   c) 11:4   d) 5:1   e) 12:1   f) 60:5

Answer [   ]

17 a) 11:100   b) 8:1   c) 10:1   d) 9:99   e) 22:1   f) 111:99
     g) 3:27   h) 254:64   i) 32:2   j) 16:128   k) 3:7

Answer [   ]

18 a) 35:3   b) 14:2   c) 24:8   d) 15:3   e) 17:2   f) 38:3
     g) 34:4   h) 5:27   i) 4:33   j) 6:10   k) 1:6

Answer [   ]

19 a) 14:3   b) 19:6   c) 11:32   d) 17:26   e) 6:3   f) 7:3
     g) 7:2   h) 3:4   i) 0:3   j) 9:42   k) 7:1

Answer [   ]

20 a) 9:10   b) 11:10   c) 104:96   d) 12:13   e) 60:52
     f) 128:256   g) 48:45   h) 26:12   i) 9:4   j) 7:11   k) 13:8

Answer [   ]

21 a) 54:48   b) 16:20   c) 66:44   d) 28:16   e) 3:1   f) 3:5
     g) 4:3   h) 3:6   i) 7:4   j) 9:5

Answer [   ]

22 a) 12:20   b) 63:21   c) 8:13   d) 512:128   e) 5:1
     f) 444:333   g) 6:1   h) 153:6   i) 17:11   j) 4:1   k) 99:207

Answer [   ]

23 a) 52:26   b) 15:14   c) 14:21   d) 13:11   e) 16:2   f) 66:26
     g) 52:99   h) 62:93   i) 14:4   j) 39:55   k) 15:12

Answer [   ]

24 a) 77:11   b) 17:8   c) 19:13   d) 17:31   e) 21:20   f) 39:43
     g) 210:86   h) 88:17   i) 84:7   j) 48:95   k) 85:155

Answer [   ]

Answers and explanations to Test 6
Number logic

1	a e	2:2 is the same as 1:1
2	b c	12:6 is the same as 2:1
3	d e	6:18 = 1:3
4	a d	36:6 = 6:1
5	a d	4:10 = 5:2
6	b e	5:3 = 9:15
7	a b	18:3 = 1:6
8	b d	14:2 = 6:42
9	a f	2:1 = 4:8
10	c d	5:3 = 15:9
11	a f	5:9 = 15:27
12	a e	13:1 = 3:39
13	d f	10:2 = 25:5
14	c d	5:1 = 35:7
15	a c	8:7 = 21:24
16	e f	12:1 = 60:5
17	b j	8:1 = 16:128
18	e g	17:2 = 34:4 (8 ½)
19	a j	14:3 = 9:42 (4 2/3)
20	c d	104:96 = 12:13
21	d i	28:16 = 12:13
22	d j	512:128 = 4:1
23	c h	14:21 = 62:93
24	d k	17:31 = 85:155

Obtaining the total score

Count up the number of correct answers: _____

Deduct 1/4 of the number of wrong answers
(round down 1/4 and ½, round up 3/4): _____

Basic score: _____

Add 2 if no mistakes: _____

Test score: _____

Establishing your level of potential

Test score	1	2	3–4	5–7	8–9	10–11	12–14	15–18	19–21	22–26
Score for potential	1	2	3	4	5	6	7	8	9	10

Your scores can be used further when you get to Chapter 6.

Potential in this area could point to many careers where the analysis of quantitative data is important. Such areas might be as diverse as marketing and science, because both involve the use of statistics.

Chapter 3
Perceptual tests

Perceptual tests are often used to establish levels of intelligence in a 'fair' manner because they do not have the biases of verbal or numerical tests, which depend to some degree upon learnt skills. In Test 7, 'Perceptual logic', you have to see how an idea evolves in order to work out what will happen next.

Test 8, 'Perceptual deduction', asks you to form ideas or principles that link some things together, but exclude others. You have to see what is relevant in the information with which you are presented.

If you are able to do well on Test 9, 'Power focus', it will show evidence of intelligence that may not be revealed in any conventional way (for example, by success at scholastic subjects). When performance on this test is better than that on any other test it generally indicates that your level of academic attainment has not been fully expressed, even if you have already done well academically.

Test 7 Perceptual logic

This tests how well you make logical decisions based upon visual information. You are given a series of pictures, lines or diagrams. Your task is to see how they go together, then work out which will be the next figure in the series. You have to choose one from the four possible answers provided.

Example

Which comes next?

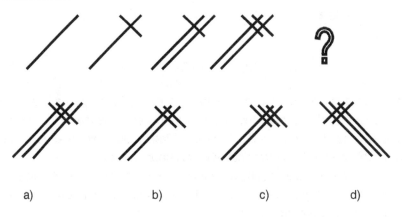

The answer is a) because one line is added each time. The long bar, which slopes from right to left, is always added first.

If you are timing yourself you have 6 minutes to do as much as you can. Put the correct answer in the box. Do not start the test until you are ready.

1   Which comes next?

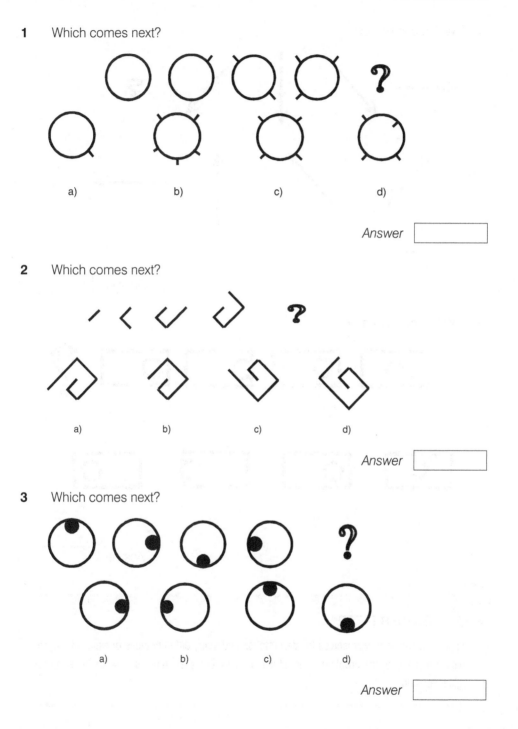

2   Which comes next?

3   Which comes next?

4   Which comes next?

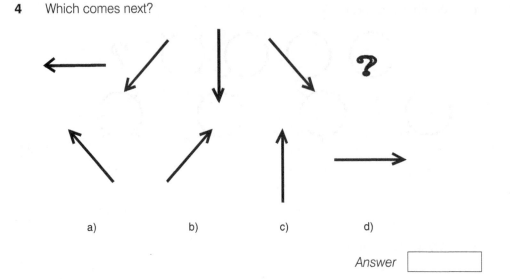

a)   b)   c)   d)

Answer

5   Which comes next?

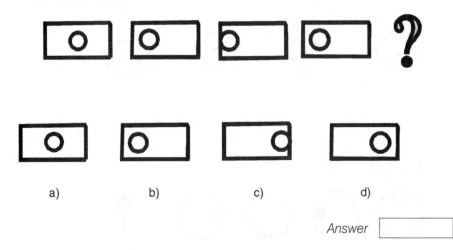

a)   b)   c)   d)

Answer

EXPERT TIP

Visual problems lend themselves to interpretation and many different types of explanation. It is unlikely that any of the problems will actually be very complex. Always look for the simplest logical solution.

6

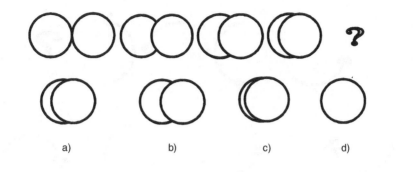

a)   b)   c)   d)

Answer

7

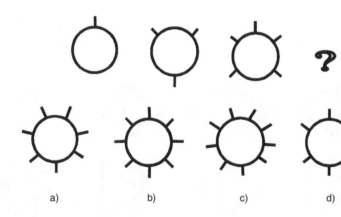

a)   b)   c)   d)

Answer

8

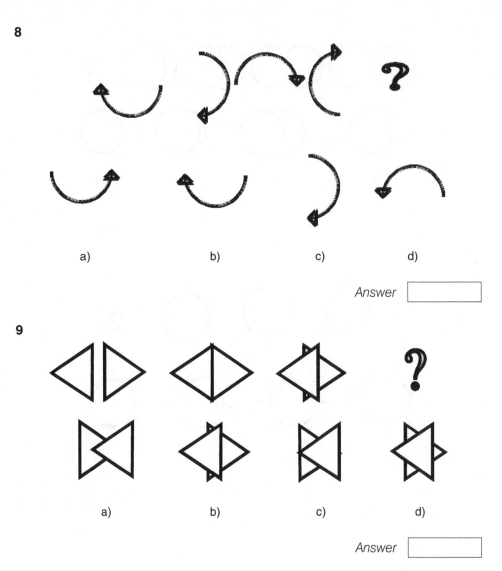

a)   b)   c)   d)

Answer [   ]

9

a)   b)   c)   d)

Answer [   ]

10

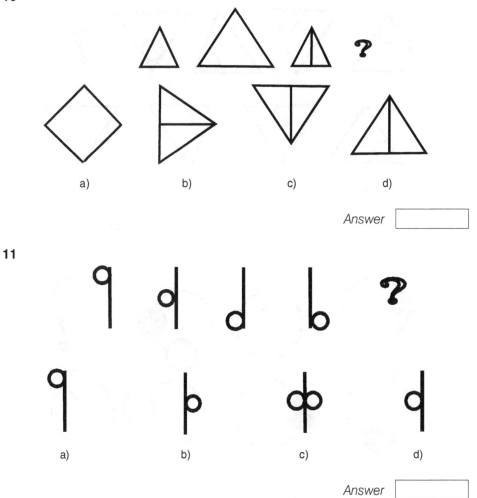

a)   b)   c)   d)

Answer [   ]

11

a)   b)   c)   d)

Answer [   ]

12

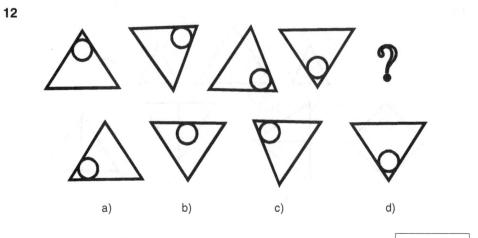

a)   b)   c)   d)

Answer

13

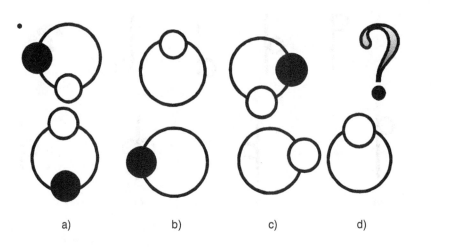

a)   b)   c)   d)

Answer

EXPERT TIP

You may be presented by an image that becomes 'hidden' or 'masked' by another image in the series. You have to hold the image in your mind while working out the rest of the problem, and mentally constructing where the image is going to emerge. In Question 13 the white circle is moving up and down while the black circle is moving around the big circle. The white circle may 'mask' the black circle where they come together.

Sometimes, as in Question 14, you have to be able to separate what happens with the image in the 'foreground' from what happens to the image in the 'background'.

14

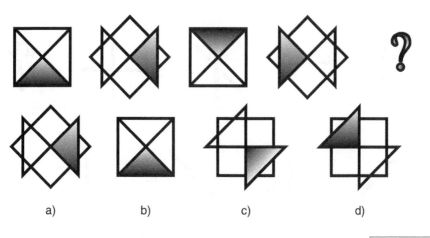

a) b) c) d)

Answer

15

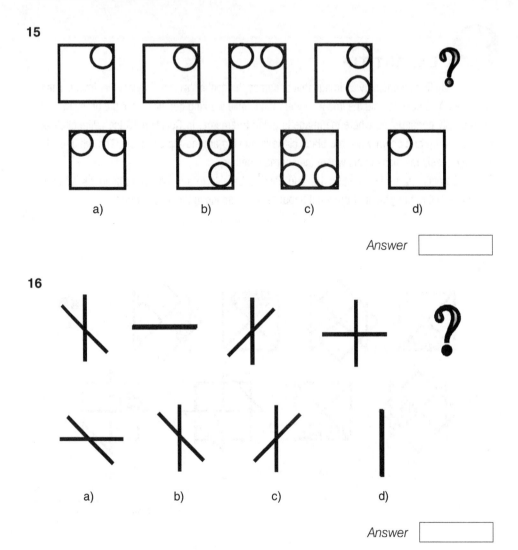

a)   b)   c)   d)

Answer

16

a)   b)   c)   d)

Answer

17

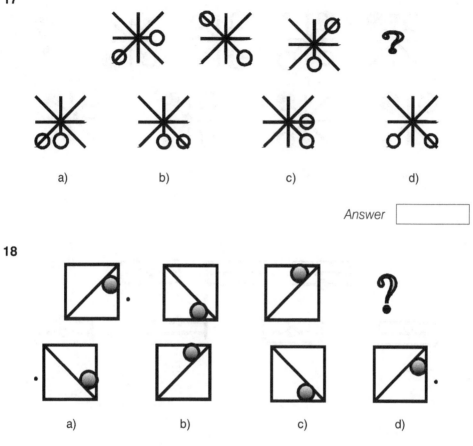

a)   b)   c)   d)

Answer _____

18

a)   b)   c)   d)

Answer _____

19

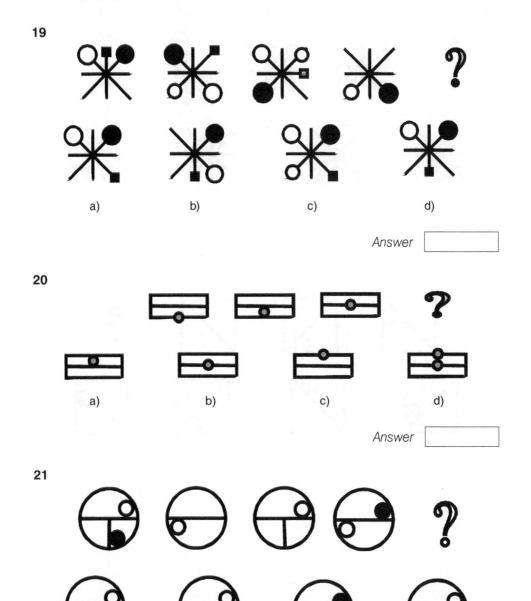

a)   b)   c)   d)

Answer

20

a)   b)   c)   d)

Answer

21

a)   b)   c)   d)

Answer

22

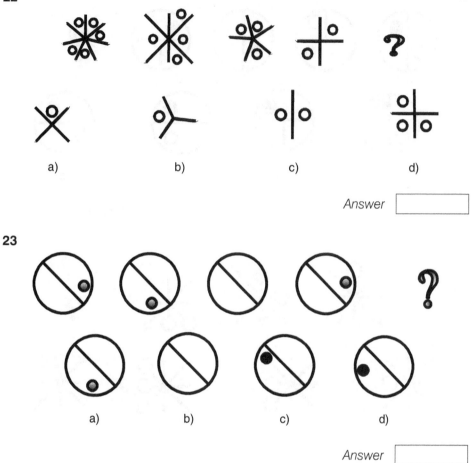

a)   b)   c)   d)

Answer [   ]

23

a)   b)   c)   d)

Answer [   ]

24

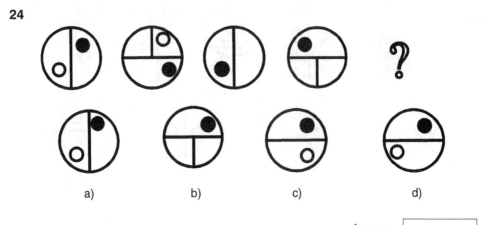

Answer [   ]

25

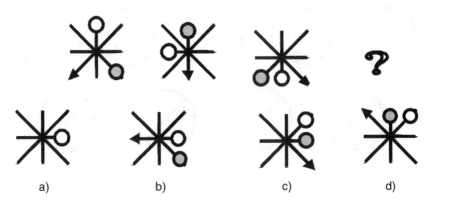

Answer [   ]

26

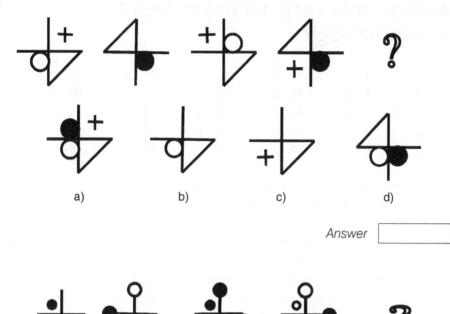

a)   b)   c)   d)

Answer

27

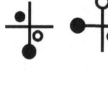

a)   b)   c)   d)

Answer

Answers and explanations to Test 7
Perceptual logic

1	c	**6**	d	**11**	b	**16**	b	**21**	a	**26**	b
2	a	**7**	a	**12**	a	**17**	d	**22**	b	**27**	b
3	c	**8**	b	**13**	a	**18**	a	**23**	a		
4	d	**9**	d	**14**	b	**19**	d	**24**	a		
5	a	**10**	d	**15**	b	**20**	a	**25**	a		

1   One spike is added each time 0, 1, 2, 3 and 4.

2   A line is added each time so that it extends further out than existing lines, hence 'a' not 'b'.

3   The small black circle moves clockwise around the larger circle at 12, 3, 6, 9 and again to 12 o'clock.

4   The arrow moves anti-clockwise from 9, 7.30, 6, 4.30 and then to 3 o'clock.

5   The small circle moves in the shape from the middle, towards the side, the side, back from the side and, next, again to the middle.

6   One disc moves gradually across another, but by how much? Answer 'c' would be only half the space travelled in the previous pictures, so 'd' is correct.

7   The spikes increase from 1, 3, 5 and then to 7.

8   The arrow is moving forward clockwise by 9 hours or backwards anti-clockwise by three hours on each occasion.

9   The left triangle successively moves towards and then across the right triangle by one third the horizontal length of the triangle.

10   The required answer is a larger representation of the previous figure.

11   The circle moves in equal stages down the line and then to the other side of the line. The most logical answer is 'b' where it has moved at an equal stage up the right side of the line.

12   The triangle turns clockwise from a side to a point while the circle stays in the same place in the triangle and moves with it.

13   In successive diagrams, the white circle moves from the top to the bottom of the large circle while the black circle moves clockwise around the large circle by one quarter. Where the black and white circles are in the same place, the white circle covers the black circle.

14   The 'back square' turns from a side to a point each time while the two triangles turn a quarter anti-clockwise.

15   A small circle is added at the top left of the square as the space becomes vacant and the additional circles have moved on around the square clockwise.

16   Two lines move across each other at their centre points. One line turns from the vertical to the horizontal on each occasion so that on the next occasion it will be vertical. The second line moves from a position that is 04.30 and 10.30, 03.00 and 09.00, 01.30 and 07.30, 00.00 and 06.00, so that on the next occasion it will be 04.30 and 10.30.

17   The circle with the line moves a quarter turn from 07.30 to 10.30 to 01.30 so that it will be next at 04.30. The white ball moves one eighth of a turn on each occasion so that it will next be at 07.30.

18   As the diagonal line changes its orientation with each succeeding figure, answers 'b' and 'd' must be incorrect. There seems no reason why the answer should be 'c' since this is the same as the second figure in the line and has been preceded by the first figure, which has a black circle beneath the line in the same way as the second figure. As the third figure in the line has a black circle above the line it would not be expected that the next figure should be the same as the second figure, which is also the same as answer 'c'. Although there is no obvious reason why the third figure has a black circle above the line, it is most logical to expect that answer 'a' is correct since it most follows the theme set by the first two figures and because none of the alternatives are credible.

19   The black circle rotates a quarter turn anti-clockwise on each occasion. The large white circle moves from 10.30 to 04.30 on each occasion and in the last figure has been covered by the black circle. The small white circle moves from 01.30 to 07.30 on each occasion and is covered by the black circle where their positions coincide. The square moves one eighth of a turn clockwise and is covered by the black circle where their positions coincide.

20   The black circle moves progressively on a line and between the lines so that on the next occasion it is between the lines.

21   There is a rotating semi-circular half 'plate' with a white circle, which is at the top and then the bottom of each successive figure so that on the next occasion it will be at the top. It covers anything else 'beneath' it. Covered on every other occasion, because it moves only a quarter turn, by the 'top' plate is a plate with a black circle. In the second figure it is completely covered by the top plate. In the third figure only half can be perceived as the part with the black circle is covered by the top plate. In the fourth figure the two plates are aligned and uncovered, since the top plate has moved half a turn and the lower plate a quarter turn. The next figure must show the top plate having rotated half a turn and the lower plate a quarter turn.

22   There are 7, 6, 5, 4 and then must be tree lines. There are 5, 4, 3, 2 and then must be a single circle.

23   The black circle moves from 0300 to 0600 to 0900 to 1200 to 0300 and next to 0600. The left hand semi-circle is the first figure is a 'plate that regularly obscures the black circle, moving as it does from right to left in successive figures.

24   The black circle is on a semi-circular 'plate' that rotates anti-clockwise a quarter turn on each occasion so that it will next occupy the left hand side of the circle. It masks the lower 'plate' on which there is a white circle. The lower plate rotates half a turn on each occasion.

25   The white circle moves a quarter of the 'clock' on each occasion. The black circle moves forward around the clock by seven and a half hours on each occasion. The arrow moves anti-clockwise by one eighth or one and a half hours on each occasion. On the next occasion all parts will be at three o'clock, the black circle and arrow being masked by the white circle.

26   The white triangle moves alternately from bottom right to top left and appears to cover any other figure that is 'in its way'. Next time it must be bottom right, which eliminates answer 'd'. The cross moves from top right to top left, where it is masked by the triangle, then reappears at top left after the triangle has moved in the third figure, so the expectation would be that, unless the cross moves on only every other occasion, for the cross to be next at bottom right where it would again be covered by the triangle. In fact, the cross moves on each successive occasion because in the fourth figure it has obscured the white circle that is moving a quarter turn anti-clockwise on each occasion. The white circle will next be bottom left. The black circle does not move and is obscured by whatever moves in front of it.

27   The large black circle moves clockwise a quarter turn and obscures the large white circle where their positions coincide. The large white circle moves on each occasion from the bottom to the top of the figure. The small black circle moves diagonally across the lines and obscures the small white circle where their positions coincide. The small white circle remains twice in the same position.

Obtaining the total score

Count up the number of correct answers: _____
Deduct 1/3 of the number of wrong answers
(round down 1/3, round up 2/3):   _____
Basic score: _____
Add 2 if no mistakes: _____
Test score: _____

Establishing your level of potential

Test score	1	2–3	4–6	7–9	10–12	13–15	16–18	19–21	22–24	25–29
Score for potential	1	2	3	4	5	6	7	8	9	10

Your scores can be used further when you get to Chapter 6

Those who do well on this visual test are often good at research and ordering information, for example, in social or historical research as well as other sciences connected with biology.

Test 8 Perceptual deduction

This tests how well you make a conclusion from visual information you have been given. In one type of problem you are given an example of how two pictures relate to one another and you have to see how the next picture relates to one of the four possible answers provided. In the second type of problem you have to see how one of the objects is different from the others.

Examples

Example 1

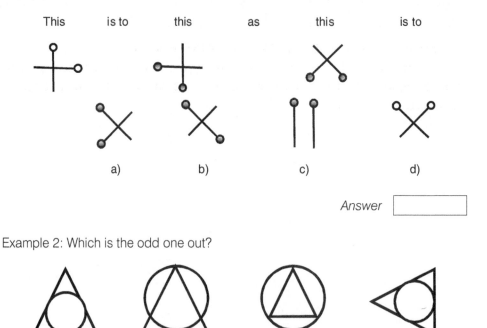

Answer _____

Example 2: Which is the odd one out?

a)   b)   c)   d)

Answer _____

In Example 1 the answer is d) because the figure is inverted top to bottom and left to right and the small circles are white instead of black in the same way as the first two drawings related to each other.

In Example 2 the answer is b) because it is the only one where one figure does not fit inside another and because both figures are the same size.

If you are timing yourself you have 6 minutes to do as much as you can. Do not start the test until you are ready.

1

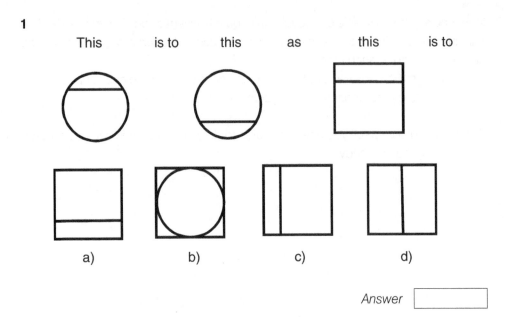

This   is to   this   as   this   is to

a)   b)   c)   d)

Answer [   ]

2   Which is the odd one out?

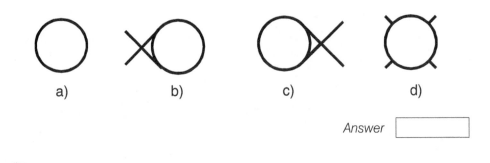

a)   b)   c)   d)

Answer [   ]

EXPERT TIP

Sometimes it is easier to make notes on the test itself, rather than use scrap paper. If you are unsure whether this is allowed, ask the test administrator. If you are working from a book like this, or from a booklet, unless you are given permission you should not mark the booklet in any way. You are almost bound to lose out if you do not follow the instructions given, especially in regard to damaging property that is not yours. If you are allowed to draw, or do calculations or whatever is necessary, do not worry what your rough work looks like: it is only your answer that counts.

3   Which is the odd one out?

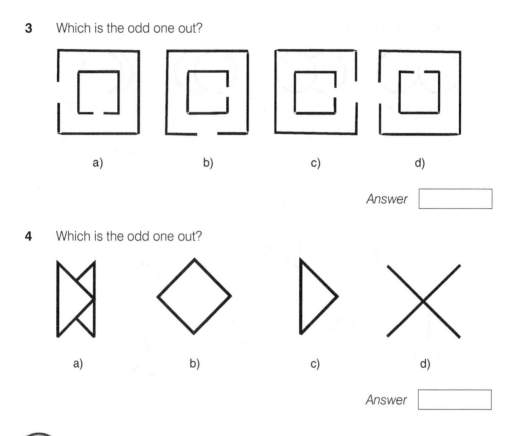

a)   b)   c)   d)

Answer [   ]

4   Which is the odd one out?

a)   b)   c)   d)

Answer [   ]

EXPERT TIP

Always look for the simplest possible logical answer. Although it is sometimes possible to say that each of the figures is odd, being different from the others, you must look for the easiest logical solution, not a complex one. For example, in Question 4, a) is the only diagram to have two shapes that also overlap, while b) is the only square. Shape c) is the only triangle, while d) is the only shape that does not fill a space. Although a), b) and c) are all 'odd' for some reason, they all possess something that makes them distinctly different from d): a closed shape.

5   Which is the odd one out?

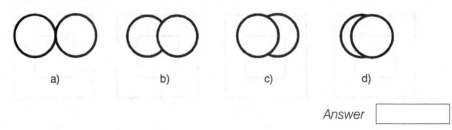

a)   b)   c)   d)

Answer [   ]

6

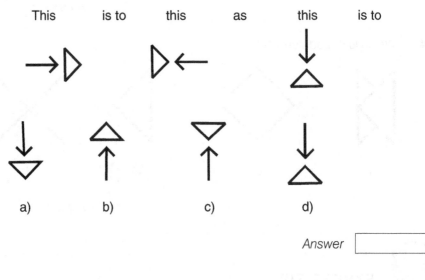

This   is to   this   as   this   is to

a)   b)   c)   d)

Answer [   ]

7

This   is to   this   as   this   is to

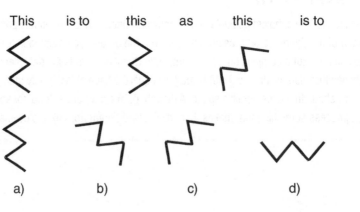

a)   b)   c)   d)

Answer [   ]

8   Which is the odd one out?

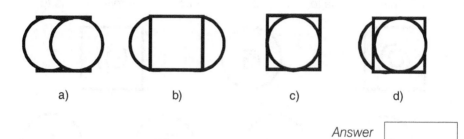

a)   b)   c)   d)

Answer

9   Which is the odd one out?

a)   b)   c)   d)

Answer

10   This   is to   this   as   this   is to

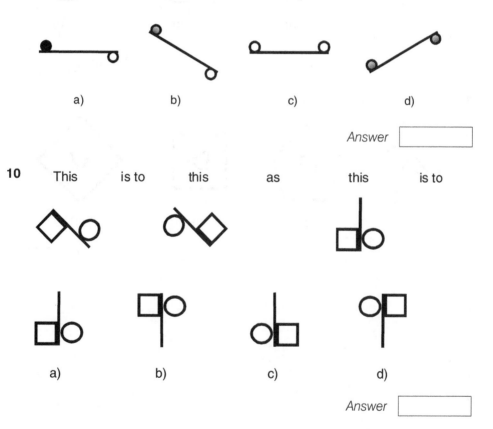

a)   b)   c)   d)

Answer

11

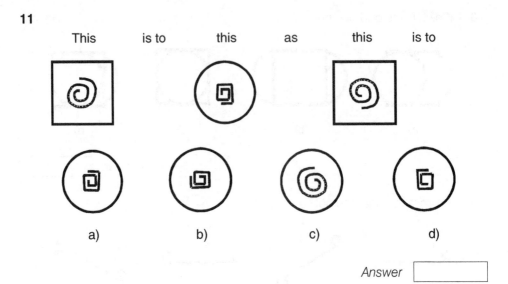

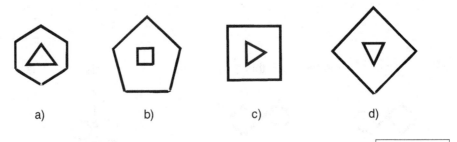

Answer

12 Which is the odd one out?

a) b) c) d)

Answer

13

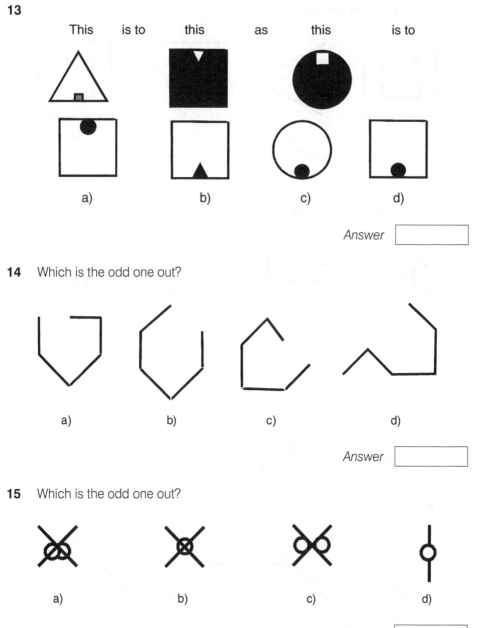

This   is to   this   as   this   is to

a)   b)   c)   d)

Answer [   ]

14 Which is the odd one out?

a)   b)   c)   d)

Answer [   ]

15 Which is the odd one out?

a)   b)   c)   d)

Answer [   ]

16   Which is the odd one out?

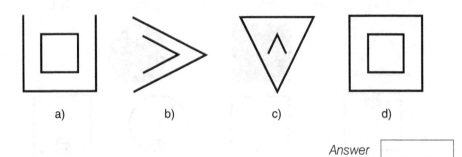

a)   b)   c)   d)

Answer

17   Which is the odd one out?

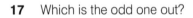

a)   b)   c)   d)

Answer

18

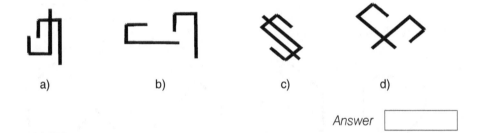

This   is to   this   as   this   is to

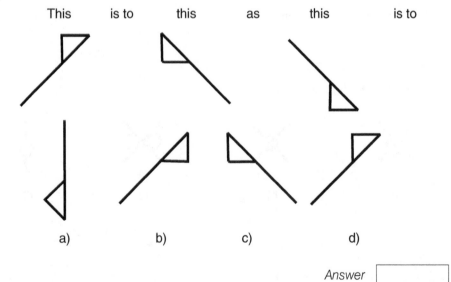

a)   b)   c)   d)

Answer

19   Which is the odd one out?

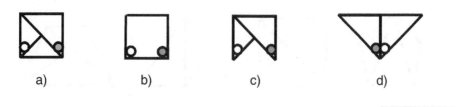

   a)   b)   c)   d)

Answer

20   Which is the odd one out?

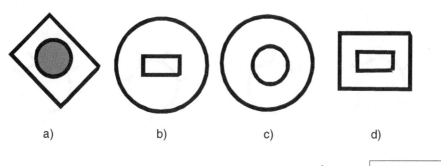

   a)   b)   c)   d)

Answer

21

This   is to   this   as   this   is to

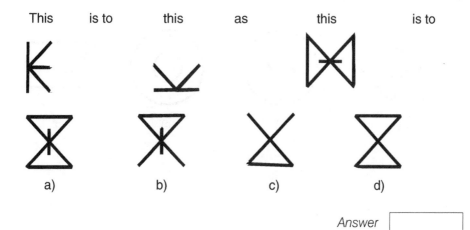

   a)   b)   c)   d)

Answer

22 Which is the odd one out?

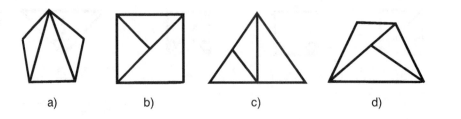

a)　　　　　b)　　　　　c)　　　　　d)

Answer

23 Which is the odd one out?

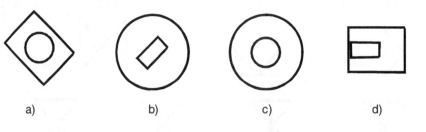

a)　　　　　b)　　　　　c)　　　　　d)

Answer

24 Which is the odd one out?

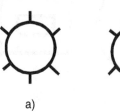  

a)　　　　　b)　　　　　c)　　　　　d)

Answer

25   Which is the odd one out?

a)   b)   c)   d)

Answer

26   Which is the odd one out?

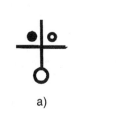   

a)   b)   c)   d)

Answer

Answers and explanations to Test 8
Perceptual deduction

1	a	5	a	9	c	13	d	17	b	21	d	25	c
2	a	6	b	10	d	14	d	18	b	22	c	26	b
3	c	7	b	11	a	15	d	19	b	23	a		
4	d	8	b	12	a	16	d	20	a	24	d		

1 One is a vertical mirror image of the other.

2 'a' is the only one not to have any attachments.

3 In 'c' the openings to the squares are aligned.

4 All, apart from 'd', are enclosed figures.

5 Circles overlap except in 'a'.

6 The orientation of the triangle remains the same while the arrow points from the base to the top.

7 One is a horizontal mirror image of the other.

8 All have a complete circle, apart from 'b'.

9 All have a circle either side of the line, apart from 'c'.

10 The figure is rotated 180 degrees.

11 A square is to a circle and a circular spiral that opens at the top is to a number of increasing lines that opens at the bottom.

12 All outside figures have one more side than the small figure they contain, apart from 'a'.

13 The small figure becomes the larger figure that now contains the previously large figure at the top or at the bottom.

14 All 'open out' by the space of a single line, apart from 'd'.

15 Only 'd' has a single line.

16 Only 'd' has two closed figures.

17 Only 'b' is un-joined figures.

18 The triangle moves from the 0130 to the 1030 position and then from the 0430 to the 0130 position.

19 Only 'b' is a figure not divided by another line.

20 Only 'a' contains a filled figure.

21 The small horizontal line has been removed.

22 Only 'c' has the same number of spaces as sides.

23 Only 'a' has an even number of lines.

24   Only in 'd' is the centre figure not in the middle of the larger figure.

25   There is one less circle than lines in each figure apart from 'c'.

26   The only figure to have four circles is 'b'.

Obtaining the total score

Count up the number of correct answers: _____

Deduct 1/3 of the number of wrong answers

(round down 1/3, round up 2/3):   _____

Basic score: _____

Add 2 if no mistakes: _____

Test score: _____

Establishing your level of potential

Test score	1–2	3–5	6–7	8–10	11–12	13–14	15–17	18–19	20–22	23–28
Score for potential	1	2	3	4	5	6	7	8	9	10

Your scores can be used further when you get to Chapter 6

This test is a good predictor of how well you can see how various things or ideas go together. This type of visual aptitude is often associated with success in biological sciences and many areas of research.

Test 9 Power focus

In this test you have to concentrate upon abstract information. Decide the picture that comes next at the bottom of each line and select your answers from the chart on page 109. The answer will always need to have two letters which reference the row and column on the chart at which the answer is found. In the three examples number 1 has been done already to show you how.

Examples

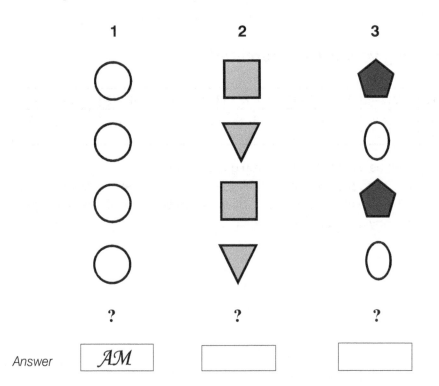

Answer   *AM*

Reference chart for the power focus test

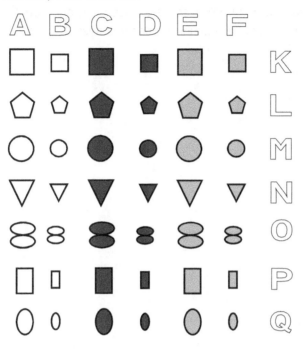

The answer to Example 2 is EK (or KE) because a shaded square is at that point when you look along the row and down the column in the chart.

In Example 3 the shaded five-sided figure appears every other time. It will appear next in line. Looking this figure up in the chart you can see it comes under row L and column C, so the answer to Example 3 is CL (or LC).

EXPERT TIP

Have plenty of scrap paper ready. Follow this rule whenever you take a test. In this particular test where it is necessary to remember more and more information, you will find it helpful to make a note of what you are doing as you work out the problem. In the case of this test, you may find it more convenient to draw any figures that need to be remembered.

If you are timing yourself you have 20 minutes to do as much as you can. You will need to keep looking back at the reference chart on page 109 as you do the test. Have scrap paper and a pencil in case you need it. Do not start the test until you are ready.

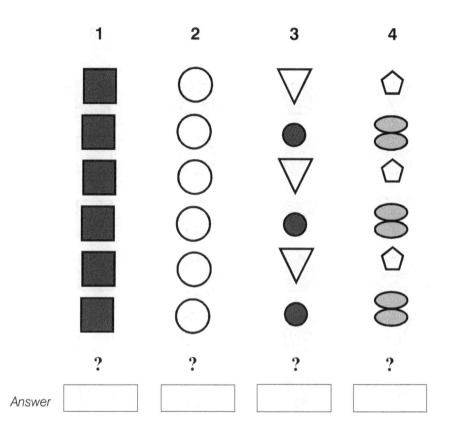

| 1 | 2 | 3 | 4 |

?   ?   ?   ?

Answer

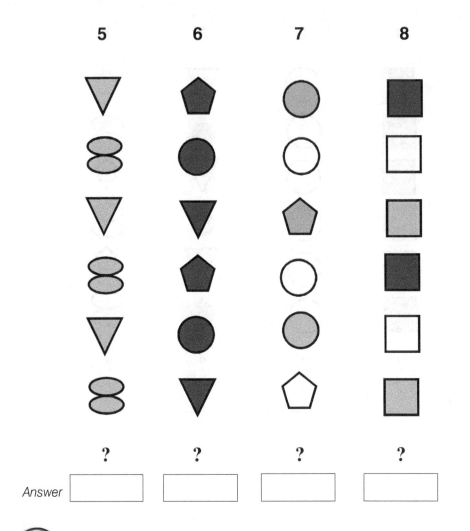

Answer

EXPERT TIP

One way to work out these problems is to break them down into parts and do each part separately. For example, in Question 7, take the shape, which has a sequence, circle, circle, polygon, circle, circle, polygon, so that the next will be circle. Write it down or draw it on your scrap paper. Then consider the shades, which are alternately shaded then white, so the next will be shaded. You now have a shaded circle. From the chart this is EM or ME.

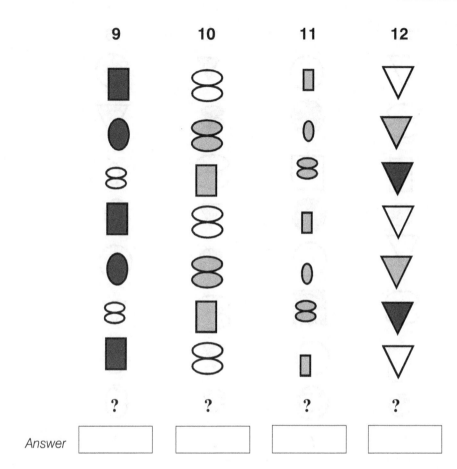

Answer

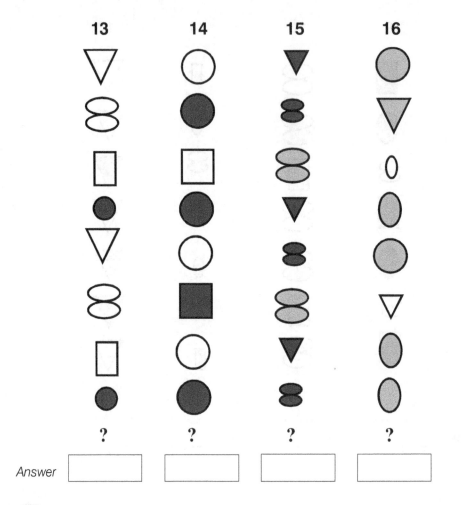

13   14   15   16

Answer

17   **18**   **19**   **20**

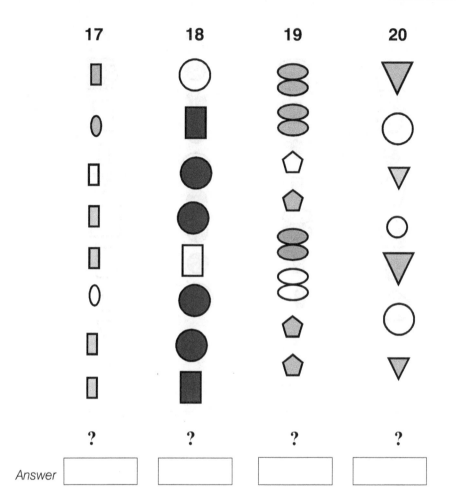

?   ?   ?   ?

Answer

21   22   23   24

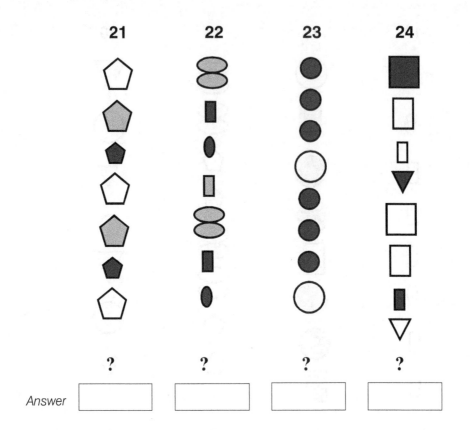

?   ?   ?   ?

Answer

25   26   27   28

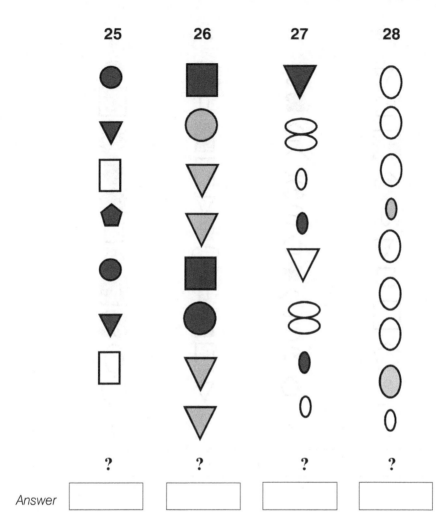

?   ?   ?   ?

Answer

29   **30**   **31**   **32**

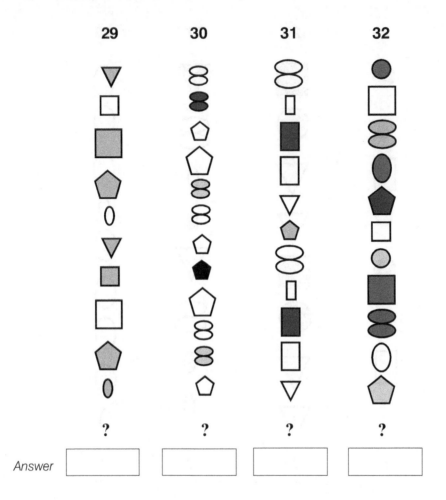

?   ?   ?   ?

Answer

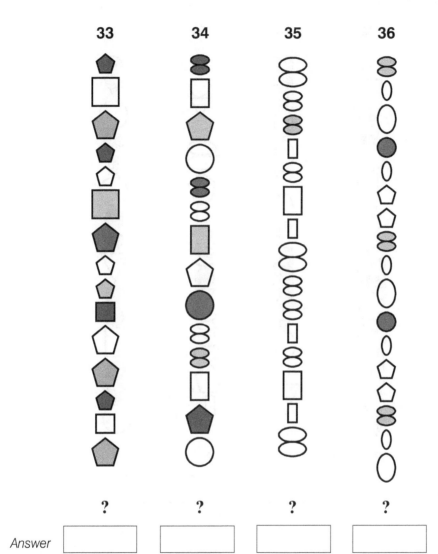

| 33 | 34 | 35 | 36 |

?   ?   ?   ?

Answer

37   **38**   **39**   **40**

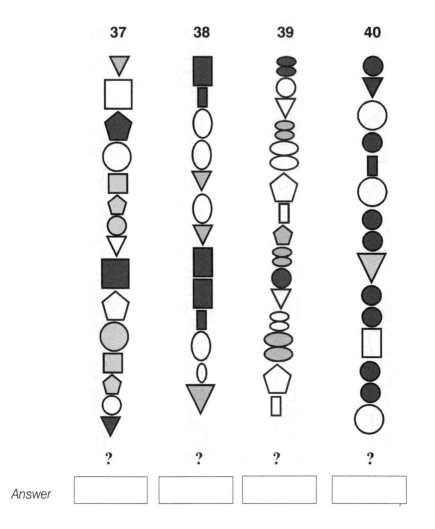

?   ?   ?   ?

Answer

Answers and explanations to Test 9   Power focus

1	CK	**9**	CQ	**17**	BP	**25**	DL	**33**	CL
2	AM	**10**	EO	**18**	AM	**26**	EK	**34**	FO
3	AN	**11**	FQ	**19**	AO	**27**	AN	**35**	BO
4	BL	**12**	EN	**20**	BM	**28**	AQ	**36**	DM
5	EN	**13**	AN	**21**	EL	**29**	BN	**37**	AK
6	CL	**14**	AK	**22**	FP	**30**	BL	**38**	AQ
7	EM	**15**	EO	**23**	DM	**31**	FL	**39**	BL
8	CK	**16**	BM	**24**	AK	**32**	DK	**40**	DN

1 With a sequence of large black squares, the next figure will be the same, CK.

2 A sequence of large white circles, AM.

3 Large triangle, small black circle. The next will be a large white triangle.

4 A small white pentagon then two joined large grey ovals repeated.

5 A large grey triangle then two joined large grey ovals repeated.

6 The sequence is large black pentagon, large black circle, large black triangle. Next will be the large black pentagon.

7 The shape sequence is two large circles then a large pentagon. The colour sequence is grey then white. Next will be a grey circle.

8 The shape sequence is large squares. The colour sequence is black, white, grey. The next figure will be a large black square.

9 The shape sequence is large rectangle, large oval, two small joined ovals. The colour sequence is black, black, white. Next will be a large black oval.

10 The shape sequence is: double large ovals, double large ovals, large rectangle. The colour sequence is: white, grey, grey. The next figure will be grey double large ovals.

11 The shape sequence is: small rectangle, small oval, double small ovals, so the next figure will be a small oval. The colour sequence is grey. Therefore, a small grey oval.

12 Shape sequence: large triangles, so the next figure will be a large triangle. Colour sequence: white, grey, black. Therefore, a large grey triangle.

13 Shape sequence: large triangle, large double ovals, large rectangle, small circle, so the next figure will be a large triangle. Colour sequence: white, white, white, black. Therefore, a large white triangle.

14 Shape sequence: large circle, large circle, square, so the next figure will be a large square. Colour sequence: white, black. Therefore, a large white square.

15 Shape sequence: small triangle, small double ovals, large double ovals, so the next figure will be large double oval. Colour sequence: black, black, grey. Therefore, large grey double ovals.

16 Shape sequence: circle, triangle, oval, oval, so the next figure will be a circle. Size sequence: large, large, small, so the next figure will be small. Colour sequence: white, grey, grey. Therefore, white.

17 Shape sequence: rectangle, rectangle, rectangle, oval, so the next figure will be a rectangle. Size sequence: small, so the next figure will be small. Colour sequence: white, grey, grey. Therefore, white.

18 Size: large, so the next figure will be large.
Colour: white, black, black, black so the next will be white.
Shape: circle, circle, rectangle, so the next will be a circle.

19 Size: large, large, small, small, so the next figure will be large.
Colour: grey, grey, white, so the next will be white.
Shape: double ovals, double ovals, pentagon, pentagon, so the next will be double ovals.

20 Size: large, large, small, small, so the next figure will be small.
Colour: white, grey, so the next will be white.
Shape: triangle, circle, so the next will be a circle.

21 Size: large, large, small so the next figure will be large.
Colour: white, grey, black, so the next will be grey.
Shape: pentagon, so the next will be a pentagon.

22 Size: large, small, small, small, so the next figure will be small.
Colour: black, black, grey, grey, so the next will be grey.
Shape: rectangle, oval, rectangle, double ovals, so the next will be a rectangle.

23 Size: large, large, small, small, small, so the next figure will be small.
Colour: black, black, black, white, so the next will be black.
Shape: circle, so the next will be a circle.

24 Size: large, large, small, small, so the next figure will be large.
Colour: black, white, white, so the next will be white.
Shape: square, rectangle, rectangle, triangle, so the next will be a square.

25 Size: large, small, small, small, so small.
Colour: black, black, black, white, so black.
Shape: circle, triangle, rectangle, pentagon, so pentagon.

26 Size: large, so large.
Colour: black, black, grey, grey, grey, so grey.
Shape: square, circle, triangle, triangle, so square.

27 Size: large, large, small, small, so large.
Colour: black, white, white, so white.
Shape: triangle, double ovals, oval, oval, so triangle.

28 Size: large, large, large, large, small, so large.
Colour: white, white, white, grey, so white.
Shape: oval, so oval.

29 Size: large, large, small, small, small, so small.
Colour: grey, grey, white, so white.
Shape: triangle, square, square, pentagon, oval, so triangle.

30 Size: large, small, small, small, small, so small.
Colour: black, white, white, grey, white, white, so white.
Shape: pentagon, pentagon, double ovals, double ovals, so pentagon.

31 Size: large, large, small, small, large, small, so small.
Colour: white, white, black, white, white, grey, so grey.
Shape: double ovals, rectangle, rectangle, rectangle, triangle, pentagon, so pentagon.

32 Size: large, large, small, small, small, small, so small.
Colour: black, black, white, grey, so black.
Shape: circle, square, double ovals, oval, pentagon, square, so square.

33 Size: 2 large, 2 small, 2 large, 3 small, so large.
Colour: black, white, grey so black.
Shape: 3 pentagons, square so pentagon.

34 Size: 3 large, 2 small, so small.
Colour: black, white, grey, white, so grey.
Shape: 2 double ovals, rectangle, pentagon, circle, so double oval.

35 Size: 1 large, 4 small, 1 large, 1 small, so small.
Colour: 6 white, 1 grey, white, so white.
Shape: 3 double ovals, rectangle, double oval, 2 rectangles, so double oval.

36 Size: 1 large, 6 small, so small.
Colour: black, 2 white, grey, 2 white, so black.
Shape: double oval, 2 ovals, circle, oval, 2 pentagons, so circle.

37 Size: 3 large, 4 small, so large.
Colour: 3 grey, white, black, white, so white.
Shape: triangle, square, pentagon, circle, square, pentagon, circle, so square.

38 Size: 2 large, small, large, small, so large.
Colour: 2 black, 2 white, grey, white, grey, so white.
Shape: 2 rectangles, 2 ovals, triangle, oval, triangle, so oval.

39 Size: 2 large, 6 small, so small.

Colour: black, 2 white, grey, 3 white, 2 grey, so white.

Shape: 2 double ovals, pentagon, rectangle, pentagon, double oval, circle, triangle, so pentagon.

40 Size: 1 large, 2 small, so small.

Colour: 2 black, white, 2 black, white, 2 black, grey, so black.

Shape: 3 circles, triangle, 2 circles, rectangle, so triangle.

Obtaining the total score

Count up the number of correct answers: _____

Deduct 1/4 of the number of wrong answers
(round down 1/4 and 1/2, round up 3/4):   _____

Basic score: _____

Add 2 if no mistakes: _____

Test score: _____

Establishing your level of potential

Test score	1−2	3−4	5−8	9−12	13−16	17−21	22−25	26−29	30−35	36−42
Score for potential	1	2	3	4	5	6	7	8	9	10

Your scores can be used further when you get to Chapter 6.

This test often reveals decision making and managerial potential, and people who do well display the ability to see through a problem, and how to deal with it in the most simple, direct way. They are therefore often perceived as the people who can 'come up with the solution' and often as the people who 'can do'. For these reasons, people with this type of talent are often regarded as natural leaders. Why such an abstract test is able to reveal talent in this way is not yet properly understood.

Chapter 4
Spatial tests

The tests in this chapter are looking for key practical as well as abstract aptitudes. In many of the problems that follow you will be expected to rotate an image in your mind so that you can 'see' what the reverse side looks like. We do this all the time in our daily lives, without giving it a thought, but psychologists have not yet discovered how a solid, three-dimensional shape is held in the mind, let alone what mental processes allow us to turn it around in our heads. It is a vital skill anyway, and one that some people are better at than others, as with most skills, which is the reason it is tested.

In Test 10, 'Shapes', you have to work out how patterns are formed and what remains when part of a shape is removed.

Test 11, 'Blocks', is a test of 'sculptural' and 'construction' potential.

Test 12, the 'Design' test, is in its nature more fluid than the previous tests. The shapes become increasingly rounded until precise definition is almost lost.

Test 10 Shapes

This test looks at how well you can see how shapes fit together. There are two types of problem. Look at the examples below to see how the test is done.

Examples

Example 1. If the figure below on the left was folded together it would make a box. Imagine the box is made of paper or card, so that you cannot see through it. On this box, a line has been drawn across one of the sides. You have to say which of the alternatives would be made from the unfolded figure on the left.

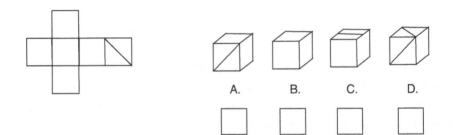

Answer 'Y' for 'yes' or 'N' for 'no' for each of the alternatives given. In the example, the answer to (a) is 'Y' for yes, and the answer to (b) is also 'Y'. The answer to (c) is 'N', because the line on one of the sides does not go from corner to corner. The answer to (d) is also 'N', as only one of the sides should have a line across it.

Example 2

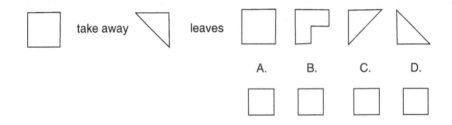

You would answer 'N' to A, as the triangle has not been taken away. Answer 'N' to B too, because if you took the triangle away from the square it would not leave this shape. The answers to both C and D are 'Y', even though the shape remaining has been turned around or over.

In both types of problem, remember that the answers might have been turned around or turned over, but still could be correct.

Answer 'Y' or 'N' to each question. If you are timing yourself, you have 6 minutes. Do not start the test until you are ready.

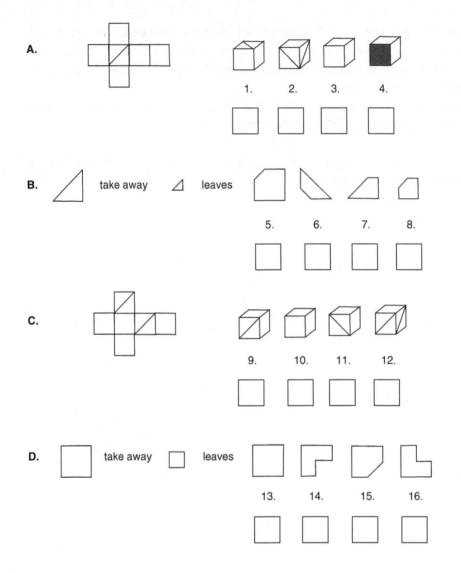

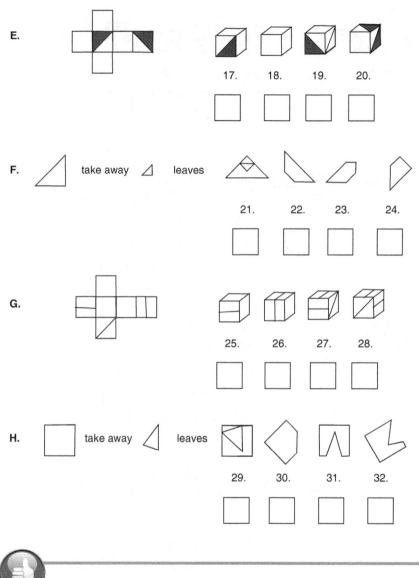

E.

17.   18.   19.   20.

F.   take away   leaves

21.   22.   23.   24.

G.

25.   26.   27.   28.

H.   take away   leaves

29.   30.   31.   32.

EXPERT TIP

You can turn the test paper around or upside down if it enables you to see the problem more clearly.

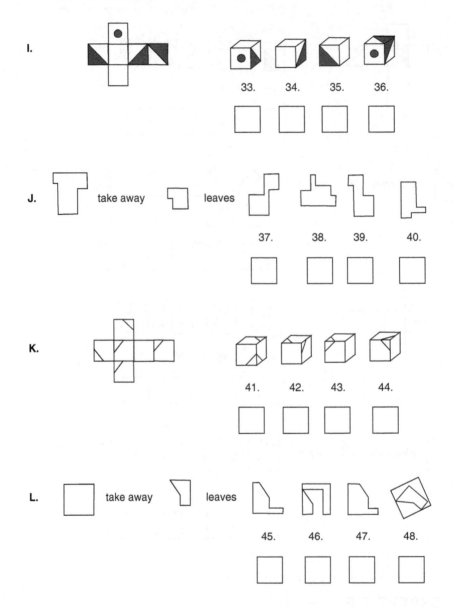

I.

33. 34. 35. 36.

J. take away leaves

37. 38. 39. 40.

K.

41. 42. 43. 44.

L. take away leaves

45. 46. 47. 48.

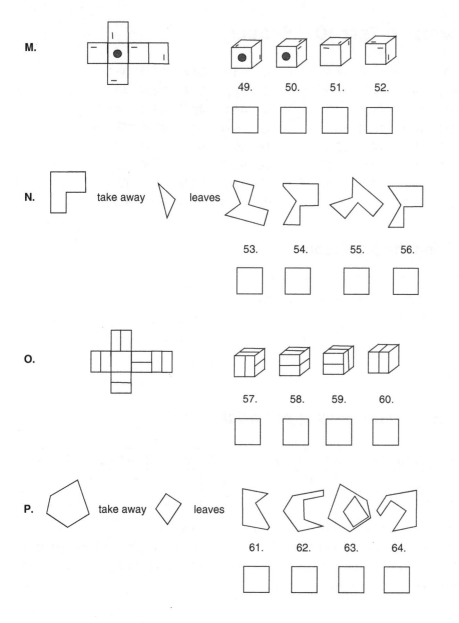

M.

49. 50. 51. 52.

N. take away leaves

53. 54. 55. 56.

O.

57. 58. 59. 60.

P. take away leaves

61. 62. 63. 64.

Answers to Test 10   Shapes

A.	1 Y	2 N	3 Y	4 N		**I.**	33 Y	34 N	35 N	36 Y
B.	5 N	6 Y	7 Y	8 N		**J.**	37 Y	38 N	39 N	40 N
C.	9 Y	10 Y	11 Y	12 N		**K.**	41 Y	42 N	43 N	44 Y
D.	13 N	14 Y	15 N	16 Y		**L.**	45 N	46 Y	47 Y	48 Y
E.	17 Y	18 N	19 N	20 N		**M.**	49 Y	50 Y	51 N	52 N
F.	21 Y	22 Y	23 N	24 N		**N.**	53 Y	54 Y	55 Y	56 N
G.	25 Y	26 N	27 N	28 N		**O.**	57 Y	58 N	59 Y	60 Y
H.	29 N	30 N	31 Y	32 Y		**P.**	61 N	62 N	63 Y	64 Y

Obtaining the total score

Count up the number of correct answers: _____

Deduct 1/2 of the number of wrong answers
(round down 1/2): _____

Basic score: _____

Add 2 if no mistakes: _____

Test score: _____

Establishing your level of potential

Test score	1–6	7–12	13–18	19–25	26–32	33–39	40–46	47–52	53–57	58–66
Score for potential	1	2	3	4	5	6	7	8	9	10

Your scores can be used further when you get to Chapter 6.

These 'putting together' and 'assembly' skills are essential with constructing forms in both two and three dimensions. They are fundamental to a range of careers in engineering and technology.

Test 11 Blocks

In this test you have to count how many times the sides, or faces, of a block touches the sides or faces of other blocks. All the blocks are the same size. Each block has six faces because the ends of the block also count as faces. Blocks that connect only at the edges or at corners do not count.

In the space provided, you have to write in the number of faces touched by each of the blocks. In the example below, the answer for block A has been given already to show you how. Complete the answers for the other blocks, B, C and D. Then read the explanation to make sure you understand what you have to do in this test.

Example

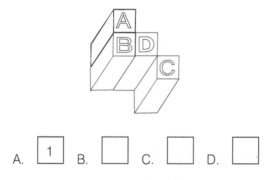

A. ☐ 1 B. ☐ C. ☐ D. ☐

Block A touches only the face, or side, of block B, but no other blocks, so the answer is '1'.

Block B faces block A and block D, so you should have given the answer '2'. Block C only touches block D at the edge, or corner, so the answer for block C is '0'. The answer for block D is '1' because it faces the side of B.

Note: Contact at the 'corners' of the blocks does not count — it must be a flat side, end or face.

If you are timing yourself you have 5 minutes to do as many as you can. Do not start the test until you are ready.

1

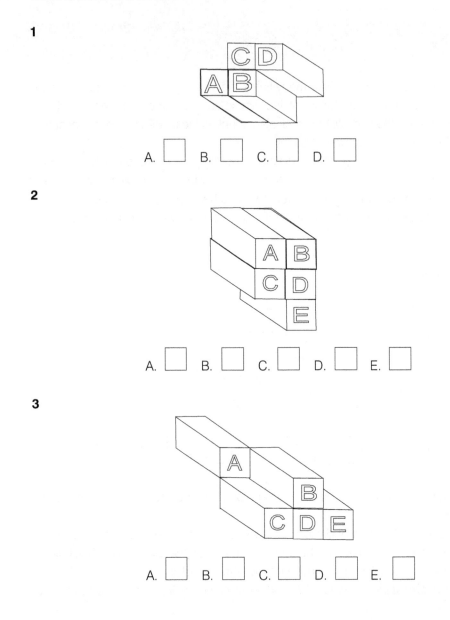

A. ☐   B. ☐   C. ☐   D. ☐

2

A. ☐   B. ☐   C. ☐   D. ☐   E. ☐

3

A. ☐   B. ☐   C. ☐   D. ☐   E. ☐

4

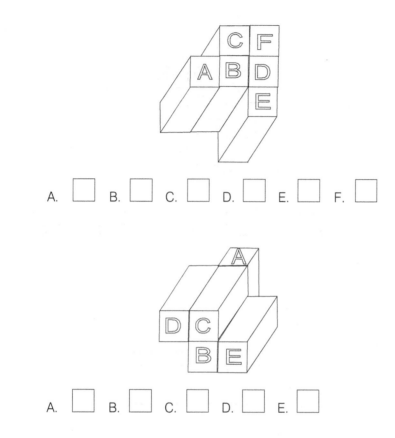

A. ☐ B. ☐ C. ☐ D. ☐ E. ☐ F. ☐

5

A. ☐ B. ☐ C. ☐ D. ☐ E. ☐

EXPERT TIP

With this type of test you either 'see' the answer easily or not. As there is no proper working out to do, apart from counting the number of sides, it wastes time to draw the figure yourself. The quickest way to do the test is simply to count as you go along.

Many people do not do as well as they could on this test because they spend too much time on checking. If you make a careful count as you proceed, checking will rarely be necessary, while a very occasional error is unlikely to count against you.

6

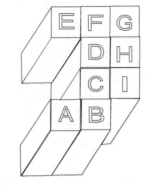

A. ☐   B. ☐   C. ☐   D. ☐   E. ☐   F. ☐   G. ☐

H. ☐   I. ☐

7

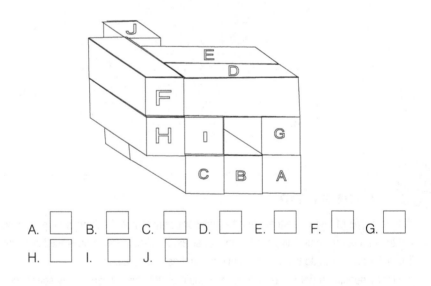

A. ☐   B. ☐   C. ☐   D. ☐   E. ☐   F. ☐   G. ☐

H. ☐   I. ☐   J. ☐

8

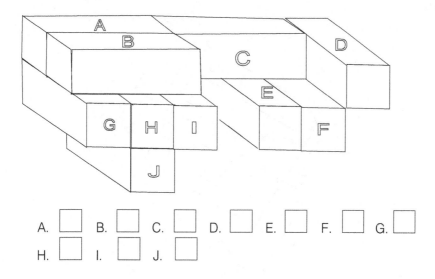

A. ☐ B. ☐ C. ☐ D. ☐ E. ☐ F. ☐ G. ☐
H. ☐ I. ☐ J. ☐

9

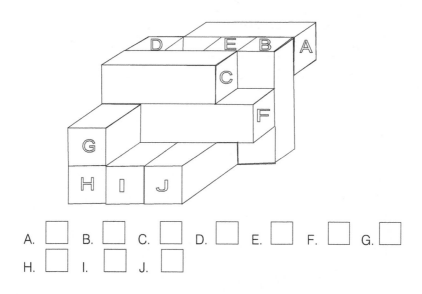

A. ☐ B. ☐ C. ☐ D. ☐ E. ☐ F. ☐ G. ☐
H. ☐ I. ☐ J. ☐

10

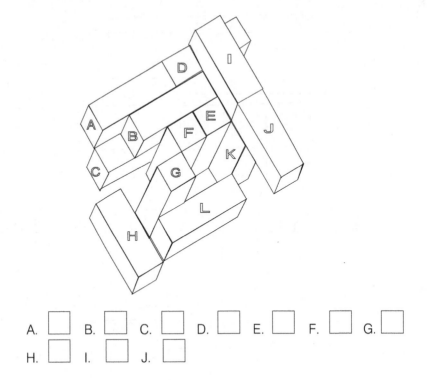

A. ☐   B. ☐   C. ☐   D. ☐   E. ☐   F. ☐   G. ☐

H. ☐   I. ☐   J. ☐

Answers to Test 11   Blocks

1 A 1, B 2, C 2, D 1
2 A 2, B 2, C 2, D 3, E 1
3 A 0, B 1, C 1, D 3, E 1
4 A 1, B 3, C 2, D 3, E 1, F 2
5 A 2, B 3, C 3, D 1, E 1
6 A 1, B 2, C 3, D 3, E 1, F 3,
    G 2, H 3, I 2

7 A 2, B 2, C 3, D 4, E 4, F 3,
    G 3, H 2, I 5, J 2
8 A 5, B 4, C 4, D 1, E 2, F 2,
    G 3, H 5, I 3, J 1
9 A 2, B 3, C 4, D 3, E 5, F 7,
    G 4, H 4, I 3, J 3
10 A 2, B 5, C 2, D 3, E 2, F 3,
    G 1, H 0, I 2, J 2, K 1, L 1

Obtaining the total score

Count up the number of correct answers: _____

Deduct 1/4 of the number of wrong answers
(round down 1/4 and 1/2, round up 3/4):   _____

Basic score: _____

Add 2 if no mistakes: _____

Test score: _____

Establishing your level of potential

Test score	1–7	8–14	15–22	23–29	30–37	38–45	46–53	54–61	62–68	69–78
Score for potential	1	2	3	4	5	6	7	8	9	10

Your scores can be used further when you get to Chapter 6.

This is the type of test that has been used as one way of establishing a talent for architecture and engineering, which require various operations of forming, molding and modelling.

Test 12 Design

This test explores how easily you can 'see' and turn around objects in space.

You are shown a shape in the middle of the page. Below it are five other shapes. Each of these is numbered. You have to decide whether each of the alternatives is *identical* to the original shape. Each one of the shapes might be the original shape, but turned around and possibly also turned over. It must be the same height and thickness to qualify as a version of the original shape.

Answer each question with a 'Y' for 'yes' or 'N' for 'no'. Try to 'see' the result in your mind. The first example has been done for you.

Example

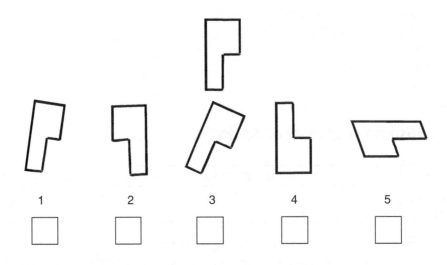

| 1 | 2 | 3 | 4 | 5 |

The answers to the example items are 1N, 2N, 3Y, 4Y and 5N.

Work as quickly and accurately as you can. If you are timing yourself you have 10 minutes. Do not start the test until you are ready.

A.

B.

C.

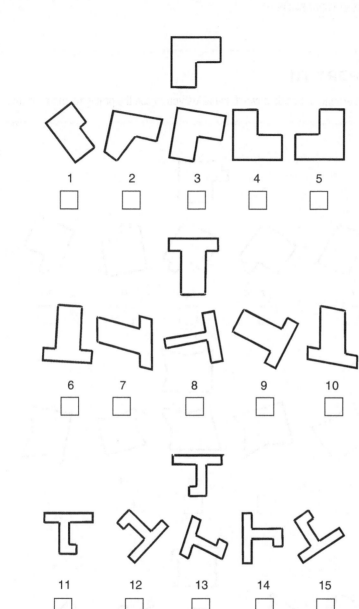

EXPERT TIP

Turn the page around or upside down if it enables you to see the problems more clearly.

D.

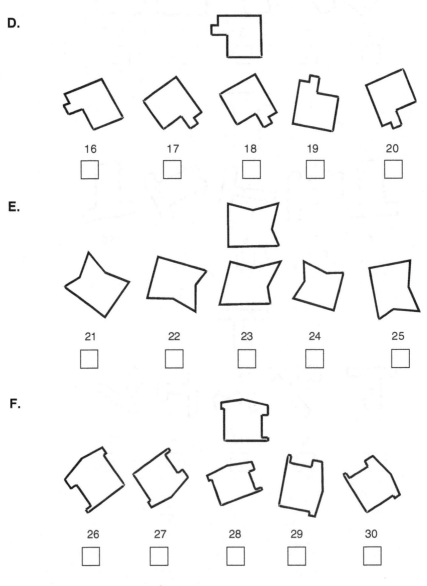

16	17	18	19	20
☐	☐	☐	☐	☐

E.

21	22	23	24	25
☐	☐	☐	☐	☐

F.

26	27	28	29	30
☐	☐	☐	☐	☐

EXPERT TIP

If you do not 'see' the answer quickly you may be tempted to guess, but this will count against you. It is better to leave out an item you are unsure of. You will not be penalized for omitting items. It is the final score that is important.

G.

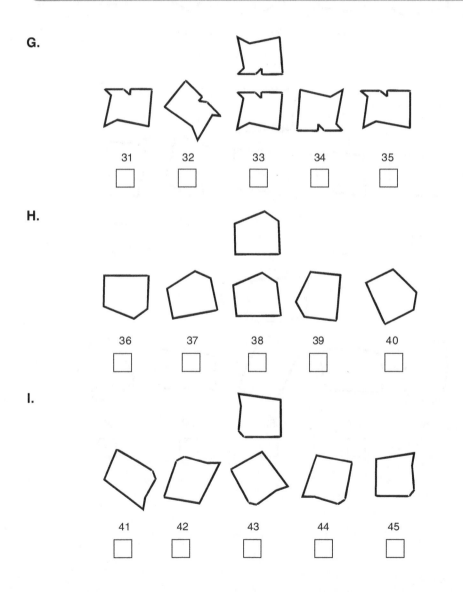

| 31 | 32 | 33 | 34 | 35 |
| □ | □ | □ | □ | □ |

H.

| 36 | 37 | 38 | 39 | 40 |
| □ | □ | □ | □ | □ |

I.

| 41 | 42 | 43 | 44 | 45 |
| □ | □ | □ | □ | □ |

J.

K.

L.

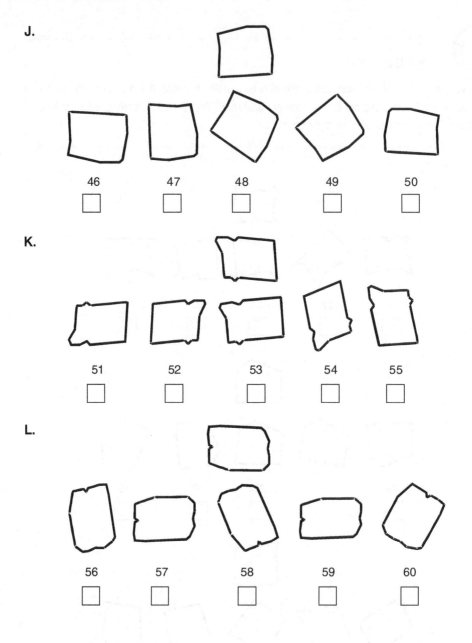

46 ☐   47 ☐   48 ☐   49 ☐   50 ☐

51 ☐   52 ☐   53 ☐   54 ☐   55 ☐

56 ☐   57 ☐   58 ☐   59 ☐   60 ☐

M.

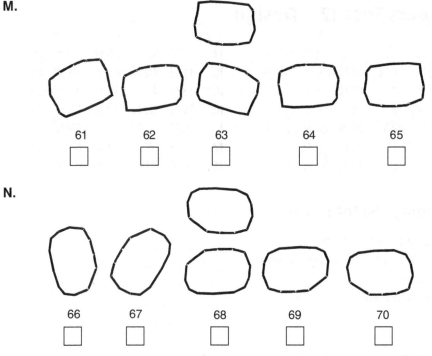

61 ☐   62 ☐   63 ☐   64 ☐   65 ☐

N.

66 ☐   67 ☐   68 ☐   69 ☐   70 ☐

Answers Test 12   Design

A.	1 N	2 N	3 Y	4 Y	5 Y
B.	6 Y	7 N	8 N	9 Y	10 N
C.	11 Y	12 N	13 N	14 Y	15 Y
D.	16 N	17 Y	18 Y	19 Y	20 Y
E.	21 Y	22 Y	23 N	24 N	25 Y
F.	26 N	27 Y	28 N	29 N	30 Y
G.	31 N	32 N	33 N	34 N	35 N

H.	36 Y	37 Y	38 N	39 Y	40 Y
I.	41 N	42 N	43 Y	44 Y	45 N
J.	46 N	47 Y	48 N	49 Y	50 N
K.	51 N	52 N	53 N	54 N	55 Y
L.	56 N	57 Y	58 Y	59 N	60 N
M.	61 N	62 N	63 Y	64 Y	65 Y
N.	66 Y	67 N	68 Y	69 Y	70 N

Obtaining the total score

Count up the number of correct answers: _____

Deduct the number of wrong answers: _____

Basic score: _____

Add 2 if no mistakes: _____

Test score: _____

Establishing your level of potential

Test score	1–6	7–13	14–20	21–26	27–33	34–40	41–47	48–54	55–62	63–72
Score for potential	1	2	3	4	5	6	7	8	9	10

Your scores can be used further when you get to Chapter 6.

If you do well on this test you must have a talent for design visualization that has probably emerged already in some artistic way. This potential can be used in many areas of study and work. These range from art and design work itself, to almost any kind of problem where information has to be fitted together to create a final picture. This is why many people who work in web design, for example, have this talent.

Chapter 5
Practical tests

This chapter is intended to prepare you for tests that investigate some specific abilities.

Test 13, 'Word order', demands that you use the alphabet. What is also being measured is how well you can maintain your concentration.

Test 14, 'Numerical systems', looks at the basic numerical skills of addition, subtraction, multiplication and division. At the same time, you have to substitute symbols for numbers, thus making the task more complex.

In Test 15, 'Graphs, tables and charts', your ability to interpret information from a diagram or list is being assessed.

Test 16, 'Memory', requires you to concentrate on a number of items and then to remember as many as possible. The test is in three parts, to enable you to see whether you are more proficient with words, numbers or pictures.

Practice on all of the tests in this chapter can improve your performance.

Test 13 Word order

This is a test of how quickly you are able to use the alphabet. You are given a list of names. Your task is to decide which one comes first in alphabetical order and which one comes last. Look at the example to see how you are to give your answer.

Examples

Example 1

	List of names	Alphabetical order	
		First	**Last**
A	Cole	A	A
B	Booker	<u>B</u>	B
C	John	C	C
D	Graft	D	D
E	Zimmer	E	<u>E</u>
F	Munny	F	F

In Example 1 the letter 'B' has been underlined because this is the first in alphabetical order. Alphabetically, 'Booker' comes before any of the other names. The letter 'E' has been underlined because this is the last in alphabetical order. The answer is 'B' and 'E'. Both letters must be marked correctly to score a point. Do the next example yourself.

Example 2

	List of names	Alphabetical order	
		First	**Last**
A	Chase	A	A
B	Friend	B	B
C	Foster	C	C
D	Moby	D	D
E	Muerte	E	E
F	Challenor	F	F

In Example 2, 'Challenor' comes first alphabetically and 'Muerte' comes last. You should have marked 'F' and 'E' with an underline, tick or circle. You must get both letters correct and also in the correct order to score a point.

If you are timing yourself you have 5 minutes to do as many as you can. Do not start the test until you are ready.

EXPERT TIP

Remember not to guess; accuracy is what is being looked for and this may be more important than the overall total.

	List of names	Alphabetical order	
1		**First**	**Last**
A	Monte	A	A
B	Avery	B	B
C	Caute	C	C
D	Strong	D	D
E	Halley	E	E
F	Doppel	F	F
2		**First**	**Last**
A	Attfield	A	A
B	Fome	B	B
C	Paste	C	C
D	Roomer	D	D
E	Caster	E	E
F	Zene	F	F
3		**First**	**Last**
A	Moncado	A	A
B	Frost	B	B
C	Prewer	C	C
D	Stirling	D	D
E	Haven	E	E
F	Bird	F	F
4		**First**	**Last**
A	Badrucin	A	A
B	Elmore	B	B
C	Priest	C	C
D	Moreau	D	D
E	Burgess	E	E
F	Bevan	F	F
5		**First**	**Last**
A	Sater	A	A
B	Stenson	B	B
C	Trewer	C	C
D	Magee	D	D
E	Hollister	E	E
F	Huckister	F	F

6		**First**	**Last**
A	Wheeler	A	A
B	Wells	B	B
C	Sorrell	C	C
D	Reed	D	D
E	Reid	E	E
F	White	F	F

7		**First**	**Last**
A	Florry	A	A
B	Forcett	B	B
C	Fostbinder	C	C
D	Cabby	D	D
E	Carney	E	E
F	Cash	F	F

8		**First**	**Last**
A	Mony	A	A
B	Millicent	B	B
C	Mauleverer	C	C
D	Maughton	D	D
E	Naughton	E	E
F	Mede	F	F

9		**First**	**Last**
A	Reynolds	A	A
B	Revnell	B	B
C	Tolly	C	C
D	Singer	D	D
E	Troll	E	E
F	Raspe	F	F

10		**First**	**Last**
A	Sund	A	A
B	Suthar	B	B
C	Suggett	C	C
D	Solly	D	D
E	Swift	E	E
F	Suarez	F	F

11		**First**	**Last**
A	Collis	A	A
B	Coleman	B	B
C	Clebatch	C	C
D	Colman	D	D
E	Clutch	E	E
F	Cliffe	F	F

12		**First**	**Last**
A	Hutton	A	A
B	Hunjan	B	B
C	Hunton	C	C
D	Hutten	D	D
E	Hushiar	E	E
F	Hunte	F	F

13		**First**	**Last**
A	Mongal	A	A
B	Moores	B	B
C	Morby	C	C
D	Mordecai	D	D
E	Moncur	E	E
F	Moon	F	F

14		**First**	**Last**
A	Tailor	A	A
B	Tennock	B	B
C	Teal	C	C
D	Tennoux	D	D
E	Tedbury	E	E
F	Templeman	F	F

15		**First**	**Last**
A	Ageros	A	A
B	Aglen	B	B
C	Adorah	C	C
D	Agass	D	D
E	Adamson	E	E
F	Acmed	F	F

16		**First**	**Last**
A	Carrasco	A	A
B	Canaway	B	B
C	Carniy	C	C
D	Carbonnier	D	D
E	Canniff	E	E
F	Carpentieri	F	F

17		**First**	**Last**
A	Watkins	A	A
B	Weaver	B	B
C	Webber	C	C
D	Waterworth	D	D
E	Wazak	E	E
F	Wearn	F	F

18		**First**	**Last**
A	Zeitzen	A	A
B	Zedde	B	B
C	Zederberg	C	C
D	Zeidler	D	D
E	Zbinden	E	E
F	Zames	F	F

19		**First**	**Last**
A	Slade	A	A
B	Sladkova	B	B
C	Slayter	C	C
D	Slaughter	D	D
E	Slattery	E	E
F	Slarke	F	F

20		**First**	**Last**
A	Eigner	A	A
B	Ekeledo	B	B
C	Ekineh	C	C
D	Ekins	D	D
E	Eilbeck	E	E
F	Ekoku	F	F

21		**First**	**Last**
A	Masware	A	A
B	Masters	B	B
C	Massiah	C	C
D	Masundian	D	D
E	Mathialiagen	E	E
F	Matalamaki	F	F

22		**First**	**Last**
A	Rowlinson	A	A
B	Rowley	B	B
C	Rowntree	C	C
D	Rowswell	D	D
E	Rowlott	E	E
F	Rowsell	F	F

23		**First**	**Last**
A	Leenslag	A	A
B	Leeson	B	B
C	Lefevre	C	C
D	Leech	D	D
E	Leedham	E	E
F	Leeming	F	F

24		**First**	**Last**
A	Homatenos	A	A
B	Holton	B	B
C	Homerstone	C	C
D	Holverson	D	D
E	Holyoake	E	E
F	Holroyde	F	F

25		**First**	**Last**
A	Preece	A	A
B	Prefumo	B	B
C	Premaradah	C	C
D	Prendergast	D	D
E	Prempeh	E	E
F	Premkumar	F	F

26		**First**	**Last**
A	Coppard	A	A
B	Cooper	B	B
C	Copley	C	C
D	Cooppen	D	D
E	Copeman	E	E
F	Cooter	F	F

27		**First**	**Last**
A	Doorgachurn	A	A
B	Doonar	B	B
C	Dooley	C	C
D	Doocey	D	D
E	Doomasia	E	E
F	Doolin	F	F

28		**First**	**Last**
A	Harle	A	A
B	Harewood	B	B
C	Harhalikis	C	C
D	Harland	D	D
E	Harjuk	E	E
F	Hariharan	F	F

29		**First**	**Last**
A	Quinnell	A	A
B	Quinney	B	B
C	Quinlan	C	C
D	Quintana	D	D
E	Quinton	E	E
F	Quincey	F	F

30		**First**	**Last**
A	Rattue	A	A
B	Ratcliffe	B	B
C	Ratnosothy	C	C
D	Ratclife	D	D
E	Rattenbury	E	E
F	Ratneswaren	F	F

31		**First**	**Last**
A	Whiddett	A	A
B	Whideway	B	B
C	Whidewone	C	C
D	Whigham	D	D
E	Whigiame	E	E
F	Whidwhy	F	F

32		**First**	**Last**
A	Fogelmate	A	A
B	Fofie	B	B
C	Fofeiter	C	C
D	Foggett	D	D
E	Foale	E	E
F	Foist	F	F

33		**First**	**Last**
A	Dibble	A	A
B	Dibbins	B	B
C	Dibbiens	C	C
D	Dibblain	D	D
E	Dibbiest	E	E
F	Dibblaite	F	F

34		**First**	**Last**
A	Gopalakrishnin	A	A
B	Gopaul	B	B
C	Gorden	C	C
D	Gorczynska	D	D
E	Gopisepti	E	E
F	Gopinath	F	F

35		**First**	**Last**
A	Kineard	A	A
B	Kindersley	B	B
C	Kinchin	C	C
D	Kinane	D	D
E	Kimpuani	E	E
F	Kimnell	F	F

36		**First**	**Last**
A	Matcheswala	A	A
B	Mastropietro	B	B
C	Masundian	C	C
D	Maswaure	D	D
E	Matatodes	E	E
F	Matembeka	F	F

37		**First**	**Last**
A	Sopitt	A	A
B	Sorgugu	B	B
C	Sopwith	C	C
D	Soreling	D	D
E	Sornarih	E	E
F	Sorensen	F	F

38		**First**	**Last**
A	Odumangani	A	A
B	Oestmann	B	B
C	Offergelt	C	C
D	Oesterreicher	D	D
E	Odyseous	E	E
F	Oducuwhy	F	F

39		**First**	**Last**
A	Patient	A	A
B	Patience	B	B
C	Pathience	C	C
D	Patil	D	D
E	Patocka	E	E
F	Patiel	F	F

40		**First**	**Last**
A	Herbert	A	A
B	Herapath	B	B
C	Heraud	C	C
D	Hentenaar	D	D
E	Heptinstall	E	E
F	Heppelthwaite	F	F

Answers to Test 13   Word order

1 BD	**11** CD	**21** CE	**31** AE
2 AF	**12** BA	**22** BD	**32** EF
3 FD	**13** ED	**23** DC	**33** CA
4 AC	**14** AD	**24** FC	**34** AC
5 EC	**15** FB	**25** AD	**35** FA
6 DF	**16** BA	**26** BA	**36** BF
7 DC	**17** DC	**27** DA	**37** AE
8 DE	**18** FA	**28** BA	**38** FC
9 FE	**19** AC	**29** FE	**39** CE
10 DE	**20** AF	**30** DA	**40** DA

Obtaining the total score

Count up the number of correct answers: _____

Add 2 if no mistakes: _____

Test score: _____

Establishing your level of potential

Test score	1–2	3–4	5–8	9–12	13–16	17–20	21–24	25–27	28–33	34–42
Score for potential	1	2	3	4	5	6	7	8	9	10

Your scores can be used further when you get to Chapter 6.

Test 13 is regarded as a good predictor of orderliness with administrative tasks, but looks in a broader way at habits of accuracy and attention to detail.

Test 14 Numerical systems

In this test you are given information in the form of symbols. The symbols represent numbers. You have to work out different sums by adding, subtracting, multiplying and dividing. You then have to choose the symbols that represent the correct answer. The first example will show you how, then do the other examples yourself.

Examples

Example 1. If these symbols represent the numbers below them:

♏︎	◹	◆	☻	♋︎	♑︎	♍︎	♌︎	♒︎	☺
1	2	3	4	5	6	7	8	9	0

then the answer to the sum:

$$☻♋︎ \quad + \quad ♋︎ \quad = \quad ?$$

is: a. ☻♋︎   b. ♑︎☺   c. ♋︎☺   d. ♌︎♒︎   e. ♒︎

Answer   ☐ c

The answer is 'c' because ☻♋︎ plus ♋︎ represents 45 plus 5, which equals 50. The number '50' turned back into symbols is represented by '♋︎☺'.

Further explanation

☻♋︎ (45) + ♋︎ (5) = ♋︎☺ (50)

Remember the following:

+	means plus	–	means minus (or take away)
/	means divide by	*	means multiply (or times)

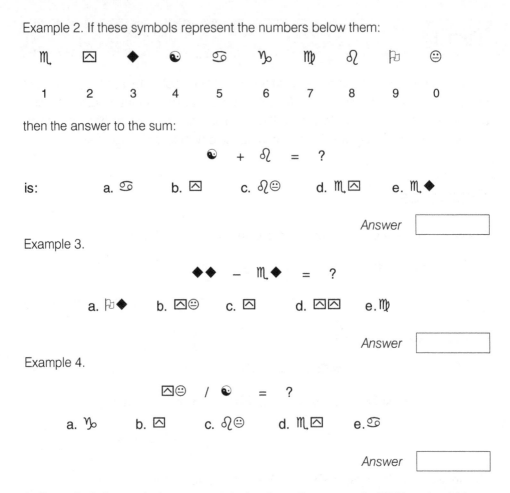

Example 2. If these symbols represent the numbers below them:

then the answer to the sum:

is:

Example 3.

Example 4.

In Example 2 the symbols represent 4 plus 8, so the answer is 12. You should have found the symbols that represent '12'. These are 'Ⅿ◿'. You should have the answer 'd'.

Further explanation for Example 2:

In Example 3 the symbols represent 33 minus 13, which gives '20'. The symbols for '20' are '◿☺', so you should have 'b' as the correct answer.

In Example 4 the sum is 20 divided by 4, which gives 5, so the answer is 'e'.

Work quickly and accurately to get as many correct as you can. If you are testing yourself you have 10 minutes. Do not start the test until you are ready.

EXPERT TIP

It is useful to be able to write in the numbers besides the symbols. This means you do not have to keep the value of each symbol in your head and makes the final computation easier. Therefore, if this is not your book, you should photocopy the pages of this test before you start. In any test, remember not to mark any test booklet without permission.

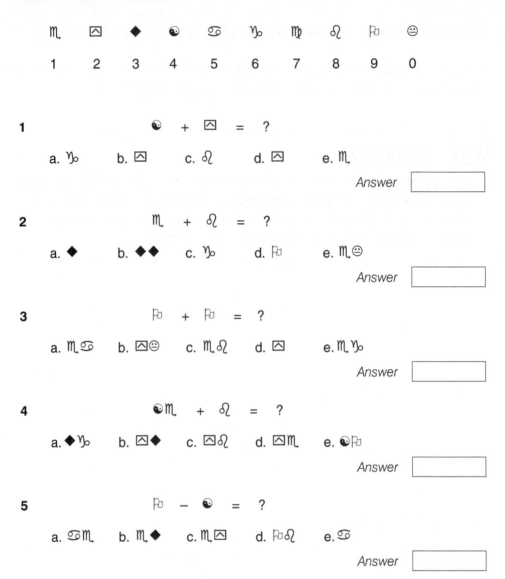

♏ ◿ ◆ ☯ ♋ ♑ ♍ ♌ ⚐ ☺

1   2   3   4   5   6   7   8   9   0

1   ☯ + ◿ = ?

a. ♑   b. ◿   c. ♌   d. ◿   e. ♏

Answer ☐

2   ♏ + ♌ = ?

a. ◆   b. ◆◆   c. ♑   d. ⚐   e. ♏☺

Answer ☐

3   ⚐ + ⚐ = ?

a. ♏♋   b. ◿☺   c. ♏♌   d. ◿   e. ♏♑

Answer ☐

4   ☯♏ + ♌ = ?

a. ◆♑   b. ◿◆   c. ◿♌   d. ◿♏   e. ☯⚐

Answer ☐

5   ⚐ − ☯ = ?

a. ♋♏   b. ♏◆   c. ♏◿   d. ⚐♌   e. ♋

Answer ☐

EXPERT TIP

Take note of the fact that some of the values of the symbols may alter in the next table.

EXPERT TIP

Do not rush through the test. Most people cannot do all of the items in the time given. Work at the pace at which you believe you are getting the items correct. Accuracy is essential.

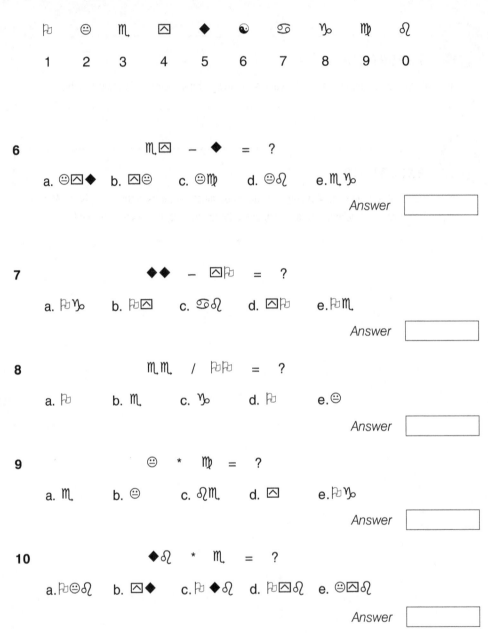

♓	☺	♏	⊡	◆	☯	♋	♑	♍	♌
1	2	3	4	5	6	7	8	9	0

6   ♏⊡ – ◆ = ?

a. ☺⊡◆   b. ⊡☺   c. ☺♍   d. ☺♌   e. ♏♑

Answer

7   ◆◆ – ⊡♓ = ?

a. ♓♑   b. ♓⊡   c. ♋♌   d. ⊡♓   e. ♓♏

Answer

8   ♏♏ / ♓♓ = ?

a. ♓   b. ♏   c. ♑   d. ♓   e. ☺

Answer

9   ☺ * ♍ = ?

a. ♏   b. ☺   c. ♌♏   d. ⊡   e. ♓♑

Answer

10   ◆♌ * ♏ = ?

a. ♓☺♌   b. ⊡◆   c. ♓◆♌   d. ♓⊡♌   e. ☺⊡♌

Answer

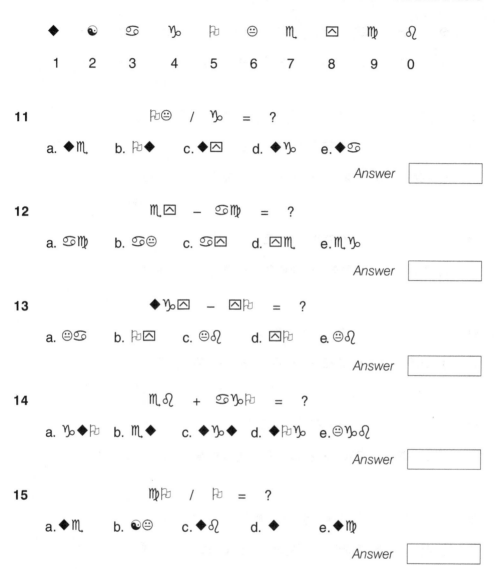

◆	&	♋	♑	○	❖	♏	⬙	♍	♌
1	2	3	4	5	6	7	8	9	0

16 ◆♋ * ♏ = ?

a. ♍♌   b. ♍◆   c. ♍♌   d. ♍○   e. ♍⬙

Answer _____

17 ◆♍♏ – ⬙❖ = ?

a. ◆♌♏   b. ◆♍❖   c. ◆◆◆   d. ◆♌♍   e. ◆♌♑

Answer _____

18 ◆❖ * ◆♋ = ?

a. &♌♍   b. &♌⬙   c. &♌♍   d. ⬙♌♍   e. ⬙♏&

Answer _____

19 ❖♍⬙ – ◆○♏ = ?

a. ○♑♏   b. ○&◆   c. ○♑⬙   d. ○♑◆   e. &○

Answer _____

20 ♋◆& / ◆♋ = ?

a. &♑   b. ◆&   c. &◆   d. &⬙   e. &&

Answer _____

♏	⊠	♍	□	♎	&	♋	♑	○	❖
1	2	3	4	5	6	7	8	9	0

21   ♋♏&□ / ⊠ = ?

a. ♍♎♋⊠   b. ♍♎♑⊠   c. ♍♎○   d. ♍❖⊠♎   e. ♍♎⊠⊠

Answer ☐

22   ○ * □♎ = ?

a. □♎□   b. □❖♎   c. □○♎   d. □♎□   e. ⊠♎♑

Answer ☐

23   ♎♏♑ / ♋ = ?

a. ♋♑   b. ♋&   c. ♋&   d. ♋□   e. ⊠♏

Answer ☐

24   ♎♍&♑ − □○♏⊠ = ?

a. □⊠&   b. □♎♍   c. ♎⊠⊠   d. □♎&   e. □♎○

Answer ☐

25   ♎♑⊠ / ○♋ = ?

a. ♑   b. ♎   c. ◆   d. ⊠   e. &

Answer ☐

Answers to Test 14   Numerical systems

1 a	**6** c	**11** d	**16** b	**21** b
2 d	**7** b	**12** a	**17** c	**22** b
3 c	**8** b	**13** a	**18** b	**23** d
4 e	**9** e	**14** a	**19** d	**24** d
5 e	**10** c	**15** e	**20** a	**25** e

Obtaining the total score

Count up the number of correct answers: _____

Add 2 if no mistakes: _____

Test score: _____

Establishing your level of potential

Test score	1–2	3–4	5–7	8–11	12–13	14–15	16–17	18–19	20–22	23–27
Score for potential	1	2	3	4	5	6	7	8	9	10

Your scores can be used further when you get to Chapter 6.

The test attempts to imitate the systems tasks that are found in many organizational tasks where dealing with information and data is important. Accuracy in this task is essential so the number you actually get right may not be the deciding factor in whether you are offered a job. Someone who is slow, but makes no or very few errors, may be preferable to a higher scorer who also makes lots of faulty judgements.

Test 15 Graphs, tables and charts

This is a test of how quickly you are able to work out facts from information given in a graph or table. You have to write down the answer. Make sure you do this clearly. Look at the example to see what you have to do. The first question has been answered already. Write in the answers to the next two questions yourself.

Example

The graph shows how many cars of different colours were sold in a showroom during one year.

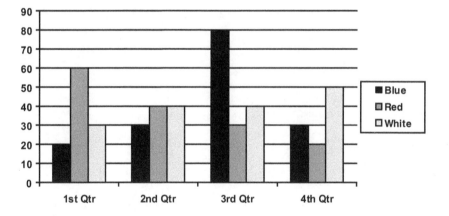

Answer

1   How many blue cars were sold during the year?

160

2   Which colour of car becomes less popular during the year?

3   In which quarter are most cars sold?

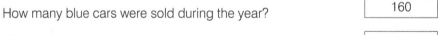

The answer to Question 1 is 160, since this is the total of 20, 30, 80 and 30, the numbers for each quarter.

The answer to Question 2 is 'red', since the graph shows that fewer red cars were sold for each succeeding quarter during the year. The number of sales went from 60 to 40, then 30 and then 20.

You should have written in '3rd' as your answer to the third question, since most cars of all colours combined, blue, red and white, were sold in the third quarter. The total for this quarter was 150, that is, 80 blue, 30 red and 40 white.

You need to work quickly and accurately. If you are timing yourself you have 10 minutes to do as many as you can. Have some scrap paper ready so that you can do any rough working as necessary. Do not start the test until you are ready.

The graph below shows the results of a survey of the way children travel to school.

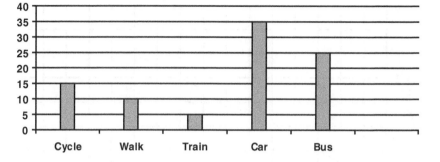

Answer

1   What is the most popular form of transport?

2   How many more children travel by car than by train?

3   How many children do not walk to school?

4   What fraction go by train compared with those who walk?

5   What percentage of children cycle?

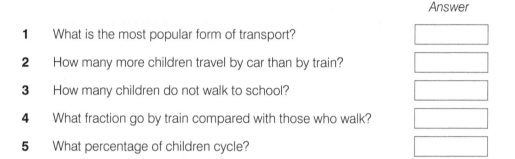

EXPERT TIP

Charts are intended to make the interpretation of information as easy as possible. In the graph above, your eye can guide you to the answer quickly. Interpreting a chart like this is usually no more than simple addition or subtraction of column totals.

The graph below converts pounds sterling to dollars.

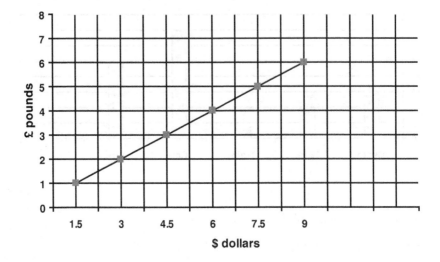

Answer

6   How many dollars would be exchanged for 4 pounds?

7   How many dollars could be exchanged for 10 pounds?

8   How many pounds would you get for 12 dollars?

9   What is a dollar worth in pounds?

10   A meal cost £26 in London and $34 in New York. What is the difference in price in dollars?

11   What is the ratio of dollars to pounds?

EXPERT TIP

'Ratio' is just another word for rate, which is generally used for currencies. The ratio of one quantity to another is the proportion that the first is to the second. Each side keeps the same proportion when divided or multiplied by the same number, so that 1 : 1½ is the same as 10 : 15 or ½ : ¼ (multiplying both sides by ten or dividing by ½).

Because of an anticipated extra demand, a bus company runs three extra buses. The timetable below shows the schedule of stops for regular buses and for the three extra buses, X, Y and Z. Where no time is given, there is no stop.

The regular service departs from the station every hour on the hour commencing at 00.00.

	Regular departure	**Bus X**	**Bus Y**	**Bus Z**
Station	00.00	14.05	14.15	14.35
Bank	00.07	–	14.21	14.42
Main Road	00.12	14.17	–	14.47
Main Road North	00.18	14.23	14.30	14.53
Theatre Avenue	00.24	14.30	–	14.59
Central Square	00.40	14.45	14.50	15.15

Answer

12   Of the three extra buses, which is the quickest?

13   If you miss Bus X at Main Road, how long will you have to wait for the next bus?

14   Which bus must you take at Bank, if you have an appointment at Theatre Avenue for 14.45?

15   If you miss Bus Z, but take the next bus, what time will you arrive at Central Square?

The graph shows average temperatures at a certain place for the first six months of the year.

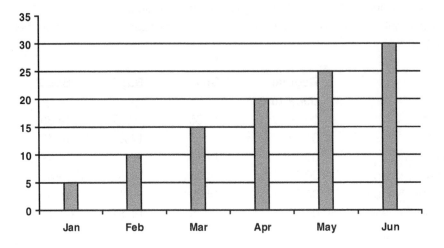

Answer

16 What is the average temperature for the first three months?

17 By how many times is it hotter in May than January?

18 If trends continue, how hot is it likely to be in July?

19 Temperatures for the months July to December were 25, 20, 15, 10, 5 and 0. What was the average temperature for the year?

EXPERT TIP

An average is found by adding together the quantities and dividing by the number of quantities involved. For example, the average of 9, 6, 7, 3, 10 and 4 is 6½.

The graph below shows the journeys of a bus, a train and a car. The increasing lines show the outward journeys and the reducing lines show the homeward journeys. The horizontal axis shows the time and the vertical axis the distance in miles. The bus and the train begin their journeys at 08.00. The car begins its journey at 08.30.

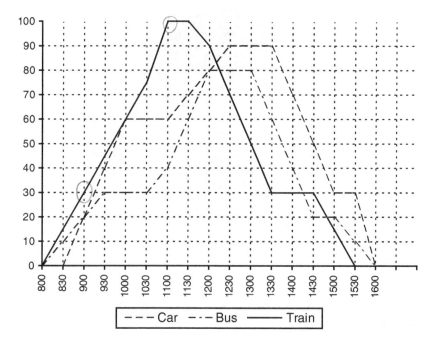

Car --- Bus --- Train

Answer

20 For how long did the car stop during the morning?

21 How many times did the bus and train pass each other?

22 What was the average speed of travel of the train from
09.00 until 11.00 including any halts?

23 How many miles in total did the car travel?

24 What was the average speed of the bus including
any halts?

The chart below shows how a government authority accounted for expenditure in different sectors.

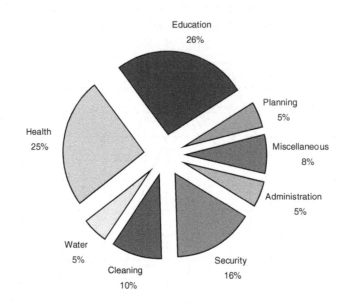

Answer

25 If the cost of Water was £4 million, what was the cost of all the services combined?

26 How much did Security cost?

27 What fraction of the total was the combined expenditure of Security, Education and Miscellaneous?

28 What is the ratio of the combined expenditure on Planning and Administration to Health?

EXPERT TIP

This type of chart is usually called a 'pie chart' (since it is a little like looking down on a cake divided into slices). It is useful as it is easy to see how the different segments or slices contribute to the total pie.

Answers and explanations to Test 15
Graphs, tables and charts

1	car	**9**	67p (£0.67)	**16**	10	**24**	20 mph
2	30	**10**	5	**17**	5 times	**25**	£80m
3	80	**11**	1.5 : 1.0 or 3 : 2	**18**	35	**26**	£12.8m
4	½	**12**	Y	**19**	15	**27**	½
5	16.66%	**13**	30 minutes	**20**	1 hour	**28**	2:5
6	6	**14**	Regular	**21**	3 times		
7	15		departure at 14.07	**22**	35 mph		
8	8	**15**	15.40	**23**	180		

1   35 children travelled by car more than any of the other forms of transport.

2   35 minus 5 = 30.

3   15 + 5 + 35 + 25 = 80.

4   10 walk. 5 go by train. 5 is half of 10.

5   The total number of children is 90. 15 children cycle. A percentage is a proportion out of a hundred. The fraction is 15 out of 90. The percentage can be found by using

$$\frac{15}{90} \times \frac{100}{1} = \frac{15}{9} \times \frac{10}{1} = \frac{5}{3} \times \frac{10}{1} = \frac{50}{3} = 16.66\%$$

6   £4 on the vertical axis meets the line at a point that corresponds with $6 on the horizontal axis.

7   The vertical axis does not extend to £10, but £5 exchanges for $7.5, so twice this amount is $15.

8 $6 exchanges for £4, so $12 would exchange for £8.

9   Pounds exchange for dollars at a ratio of 2 for 3, that is 2 parts of a pound for three parts of a dollar. One part or, a third, is about 33 pence and two parts is £0.67. The sum is

$$1 \div 1\frac{1}{2} = \frac{1}{2} \div \frac{3}{1} = \frac{1}{2} \times \frac{2}{3} = \frac{2}{3} = 0.666 \, {}^* = 0.67 \, \text{pence}$$

10   For example, £6 = $9, so 4 × 6 = £24 or $36. This leaves £2 left to calculate. £2 = $3. Therefore a meal in London costs $36 + $3 = $39. $39 − $34 = $5.

11   As in answer 9, above.

12   Bus X takes 14.45 − 14.05 = 40, Y 14.50 − 14.15 = 35, Z 15.15 − 14.35 = 40.

13   Bus Z is next to arrive, 30 minutes later.

14   Only the regular departure at 14.07 will stop at Theatre Avenue and get you there on time, for example, bus X will make you 5 minutes late.

15   You would have to wait for the regular bus, which departs at 15.00.

16 $5 + 10 + 15 = 30 / 3 = 10$.

17 $25/5 = 5$.

18   As it gets 5 degrees hotter each month, it is likely to be 35 degrees in July.

19   The total of the temperatures for the 12 months is 180, so $180/12 = 15$.

20   The car stops from 12.30 until 13.30.

21   At 12.15, 14.15 and 14.45.

22   It travelled from 30 to 100 miles, that is 70 miles, in 2 hours, so 35 mph.

23   It travelled 90 miles there and 90 miles back.

24   The bus travelled 160 miles there and back over 8 hours, so 20 mph.

25   5% was £4 million, so 10% is £8, and 100% is £80 million.

26   5% was £4 million, so 1% is $4/5 = 0.8$ million or £800,000.00, so 16% (Security) is $0.8 \times 16 = 12.8$, or 5% (4) + 10% (8) + 1% (0.8) = 12.8.

27   Security (16%) + Education (26%) + Miscellaneous (8%) = 50% or ½.

28   Planning (5%) and Administration (5%) to Health (25%) is 10 to 25, so 2:5.

Obtaining the total score

Count up the number of correct answers: _____

Add 2 if no mistakes: _____

Test score: _____

Establishing your level of potential

Test score	1 − 2	3 − 4	5 − 6	7 − 8	9 − 12	13 − 16	17 − 20	21 − 24	25 − 26	27 − 30
Score for potential	1	2	3	4	5	6	7	8	9	10

Your scores can be used further when you get to Chapter 6.

Charts are used in order to convey information in a simple, logical way; they are not designed to be problems, but are intended to be easy. What is being measured is how quickly you can read and make sense of them. This interest and ability is a vital component which fits with many numerical and administrative professions, particularly those connected with economic disciplines.

Test 16 Memory

In this test you must remember as many items as you can. You have a minute to concentrate upon a page of items. When you turn the page you have to write down as many as you can of the items you have seen. Make sure you write clearly. Look at the example to see what you have to do.

Example

Look at the following information. There are pictures, words and numbers for you to concentrate on and to remember. If you are timing yourself, give yourself 2 minutes. Time yourself exactly. After this exact time, turn the page and write down as many of the items as you can. Give yourself a further 2 minutes to do this. When you turn over, you will see that some of the items have already been written in for you to show you how.

You have 2 minutes to write down as many items as you can from the example. You can write them in any order.

bird	pen	church
____	____	____
____	____	____
____	____	____
____	____	____
____	____	____

After 2 minutes count up how many items you remembered. Check your answers by looking back at the previous page.

Do not start the test until you are ready. If you are timing yourself, do this exactly.

EXPERT TIP

Memory tests are the most critical as regards timing of all tests. This is because any lapse of concentration can drastically affect your score. For the same reason, make sure, as always, that you will not be disturbed or distracted during the critical period. This is so essential because the mind does not lapse in concentration so much as naturally begin to process other thoughts and seek other sources to stimulate it.

1   You have exactly 2 minutes to look at the following numbers, then go on to the next page. You will then have 2 minutes to write down as many as you can remember.

99   23

16

4   17   52

31

8   13   132

2   46

22   18

81   79   40

104   58   63

Write down as many of the numbers as you can. You have exactly 2 minutes.

_____ _____

_____ _____

_____ _____

_____ _____

_____ _____

_____ _____

_____ _____

_____ _____

_____ _____

2   You have 2 minutes to look at the following words, then go on to the next page.
You will then have 2 minutes to write down as many as you can remember.

rope   computer

tree   book

coat

monkey   pencil

cup   vase

carpet   chair

hat

ticket   picture

necklace   boat

baby   motorbike

glove

bridge

Write down as many of the words as you can. You have exactly 2 minutes.

_____ _____

_____ _____

_____ _____

_____ _____

_____ _____

_____ _____

_____ _____

_____ _____

_____ _____

_____ _____

3   You have exactly 2 minutes to look at the following pictures, then go on to the next page. You will then have 2 minutes to write down as many as you can remember.

Write down as many of the pictures as you can. You have exactly 2 minutes.

————	————
————	————
————	————
————	————
————	————
————	————
————	————
————	————
————	————

Answers to Test 16   Memory

Each test can be scored individually.

Obtaining the total score

Count up the number of correct answers: _____
Add 2 if no mistakes: _____
Test score: _____

Establishing your level of potential

Test score	1	2−3	4−5	6−7	8−9	10−12	13−14	15−16	17−18	19−22
Score for potential	1	2	3	4	5	6	7	8	9	10

Your scores can be used further when you get to Chapter 6.

How well you do on this type of task can give insights into whether you are able to focus your mind when necessary and also how easily you might be distracted. This type of evidence can also be useful as an indication of which area of work or study might suit you best – broadly, working with either words, numbers or images.

Chapter 6
Interpreting your test results

Your aptitude profile

If you have done one or more of the 16 tests in this book, you should have worked out a score for potential for each, ranging from 0 to 10. How to do this was explained at the end of each test. Remember that these give only an indication of potential; the tests have not been 'standardized' by full-scale trials, so the scores are not precise measures in the way that fully standardized tests are. This chapter is about how information gained from tests can be used, and your scores on the tests in the workbook can be used as examples.

If you have not timed yourself on the tests, you can use your own estimates of your potential in the charts below. It depends how far you agree that the test results are fully and accurately assessing you. There is always room for some doubt. Your results might be affected by all sorts of issues relating to:

- the efficiency with which you test yourself;

- the conditions in which you test yourself;

- who you compare yourself with;

- whether the tests themselves have reliably detected your potential.

Therefore your own estimates will be based on other experiences, and how much weight you place upon the difference between any two scores is, in the end, for you to judge.

Put marks on Table 6.1 to show where you scored on each one of the tests, and join up these points to obtain an easy to view graph. This chart will give you a rough indication of where your strengths and weaknesses lie. As well as looking at your best performance, see whether the tests group themselves in any way. For example, do you tend to do better on the perceptual tests than on the verbal ones? If a pattern is revealed, this may give you more insight into a wider range of training or career possibilities where more than a single talent may be required.

In Figure 6.1 you can see how a score on a test might be used to calculate your level of intelligence. This type of calculation is often rather academic, and may be used more by psychologists for diagnostic reasons than by employers.

In Figure 6.2 you can see how a score on a test might be used to indicate how much better you are than other people taking the same test. This type of comparison is frequently found useful by employers and other selectors because it indicates those people who are likely to require the least amount of training, or those who will respond most quickly to a particular work situation.

TABLE 6.1   Level and pattern of scores

Test 1 Word skills	1	2	3	4	5	6	7	8	9	10
Test 2 Verbal concepts	1	2	3	4	5	6	7	8	9	10
Test 3 Critical application	1	2	3	4	5	6	7	8	9	10
Test 4 Number skills	1	2	3	4	5	6	7	8	9	10
Test 5 Numerical reasoning	1	2	3	4	5	6	7	8	9	10
Test 6 Number logic	1	2	3	4	5	6	7	8	9	10
Test 7 Perceptual logic	1	2	3	4	5	6	7	8	9	10
Test 8 Perceptual deduction	1	2	3	4	5	6	7	8	9	10
Test 9 Power focus	1	2	3	4	5	6	7	8	9	10
Test 10 Shapes	1	2	3	4	5	6	7	8	9	10
Test 11 Blocks	1	2	3	4	5	6	7	8	9	10
Test 12 Design	1	2	3	4	5	6	7	8	9	10
Test 13 Word order	1	2	3	4	5	6	7	8	9	10
Test 14 Numerical systems	1	2	3	4	5	6	7	8	9	10
Test 15 Graphs, tables and charts	1	2	3	4	5	6	7	8	9	10
Test 16 Memory	1	2	3	4	5	6	7	8	9	10

The greater the difference between tests, the more likely it is that you really are better on one type of test than another. This difference may be important to you in determining the most suitable area of study or what career to pursue.

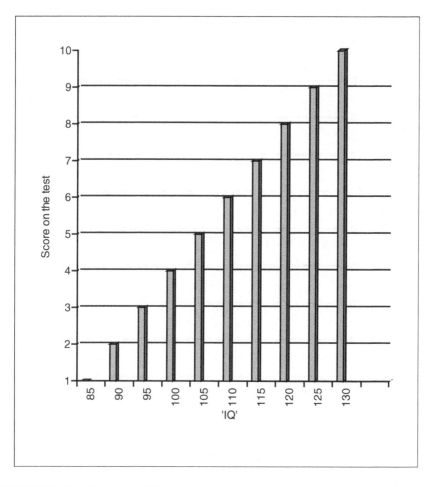

FIGURE 6.1 Score and IQ

On the IQ scale 100 is taken as the average. The scale allows estimates on each test of the relationship of your performance to the average.

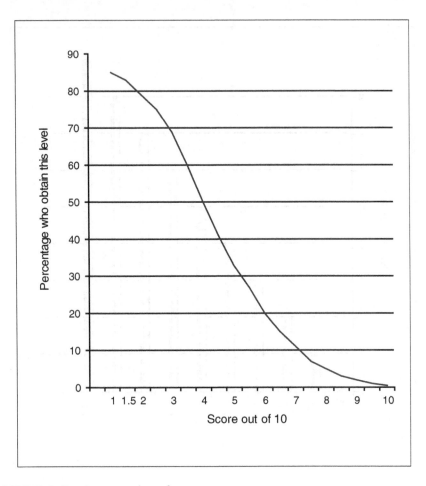

FIGURE 6.2 Score and performance

To illustrate, if you score 7 you are in about the top 10% of people on a test. To look at it another way, only 10% of people would be expected to obtain a higher score.

Your career potential

The following pages contain suggestions for careers based upon your test results. They represent broad indications and suggestions, but this is not meant to be an exact process.

Bear in mind that within each category, whether verbal, numerical, perceptual, spatial or practical, some careers are more related to one type of test than another. You may need to refer back to the opening remarks that preceded each chapter, as well as to any remarks at the end of each test, where some indication was given of the relevance and intention of each of the tests.

It is obvious that many careers can fit into more than one category. Legal work can be as much verbal as numerical; an architect requires a good sense of space, but must also be numerically competent. Also, some career titles contain many types of possibility within them; there are different functions in the civil service; the career of a designer could be graphics, textiles, stage settings, engineering and many other types as well.

To sum up, the workbook offers illustrations about possibilities, but does not seek to be specific about career opportunities. This has been done more comprehensively in *Test Your Own Aptitude*; *Test Yourself; Career, Aptitude and Selection Tests* and *Advanced Aptitude Tests*, also published by Kogan Page.

Verbal tests

If you scored well in these you could consider becoming an:

Actor	Foreign correspondent
Advertising copywriter	Film reviewer
Advocate	Freelance writer
Anthropologist	Historian
Archaeologist	Human resources manager
Archivist	Information officer
Art gallery curator/keeper	Interpreter
Author	Interviewer
Barrister	Journalist
Bilingual secretary	Judge
Book critic	Language teacher
Book editor	Lawyer
Book publisher	Liberal studies teacher
Counsellor	Librarian
Court reporter	Linguist
Detective	Literary agent
Diplomatic service staff	Literary critic
Director (media)	Press agent
Drama teacher	Reporter
Editor	Solicitor
Educational psychologist	Speech therapist
English language teacher	Translator

Numerical tests

If you scored well in these you could consider becoming an:

Account executive
Account planner
Accountant
Actuary
Administrator
Astronomer
Auditor
Business consultant
Civil servant
Company secretary
Economist
Financial analyst
Lawyer
Management consultant
Managing director
Mathematician

Merchandiser
Operational researcher
Patent examiner
Purchasing manager
Quantity surveyor
Producer (films)
Programmer
Science teacher
Securities analyst
Tax inspector
Solicitor
Statistician
Stockbroker
Systems analyst
Tax adviser
Underwriter

Perceptual tests

If you scored well in these you could consider becoming an:

Acupuncturist
Air traffic controller
Anthropologist
Antique dealer
Applications programmer
Archaeologist
Aromatherapist
Bacteriologist
Biologist
Botanist
Chemist
Chiropodist
Clinical psychologist
Computer systems analyst
Conservation officer
Curator
Dentist
Ecologist
Educational psychologist
Environmental health officer

Food scientist
Genealogist
Herbalist
Homeopath
Horticulturalist
Market gardener
Medical illustrator
Microbiologist
Nurse
Nutritionist
Occupational therapist
Police officer
Pharmacist
Psychotherapist
Reflexologist
Science teacher
Science writer
Social scientist
Social worker
Training officer

Spatial tests

If you scored well in these you could consider becoming an:

Architect
Art editor
Art gallery curator/keeper
Artist
Art therapist
Blacksmith/farrier
Boat builder
Cabinet maker
Camera operator
Carpenter
Carpet fitter
Cartographer
Cartoon animator
Chef
Civil engineer
Clothing designer
Decorator
Designer
Display artist
Diver

Engineer
Florist
Furniture maker
Illustrator
Landscape architect
Manufacturing engineer
Model maker
Photographer
Picture framer
Pilot
Restorer
Shop fitter
Sign writer
Silversmith
Stone mason
Surveyor
Teacher of art/craft
Upholsterer
Vision mixer

Practical tests

If you scored well in these you could consider becoming an:

Accountant
Administrator
Broker
Building society manager
Bursar
Buyer
Cashier
Civil servant
Currency trader
Customs officer
Elementary school teacher
Estate agent
Estimator
Financial controller
Health and safety inspector
Health services administrator
Hotel manager
Housing manager
Importer/exporter
Insurance agent
Investment advisor
Medical records officer

Merchandiser
Negotiator
Office manager
Organization and method officer
Purchasing manager
Purser
Quantity surveyor
Rating valuation officer
Retail manager
Securities analyst
Shipping and forwarding officer
Tax inspector
Trading standards officer
Post office clerk
Programmer
Retail manager
Sales manager
Stockbroker
Stock controller
Store keeper
Transport manager
Turf accountant

Succeed at IQ tests, Philip Carter and Ken Russell
Test and Assess Your IQ, Philip Carter and Ken Russell
Test Your IQ, Philip Carter and Ken Russell
Test Your Numerical Aptitude, Jim Barrett
Test Your Own Aptitude, Jim Barrett and Geoff Williams
The Advanced Numeracy Test Workbook, Mike Bryon
The Graduate Psychometric Test Workbook, Mike Bryon
The Numeracy Test Workbook, Mike Bryon
The Ultimate IQ Test Book, Philip Carter and Ken Russell
The Ultimate Psychometric Test Book, Mike Bryon
The Verbal Reasoning Test Workbook, Mike Bryon

For further information please contact the publishers at:

Kogan Page
120 Pentonville Road
London N1 9JN
United Kingdom
www.koganpage.com

The sharpest minds need the finest advice. **Kogan Page** creates success.

www.koganpage.com